Urgency.

Jeremy Vaeni

Kynegion House

Kynegion House

First Edition: March 2011
Printed in the United States of America
ISBN: 978-0-9746854-1-0

Cover Design: Jeffery Ritzmann
Printed In USA

Contents

Special Thanks

Colin Andrews for not just writing the Foreword to this book but for thanklessly speaking truth to power and having the courage it takes to keep it honest at all costs. What you have given to your research personally and professionally I can only guess at.

David Corneau for believing in this project so much that you took it upon yourself to get it seen. What an honor!

Melissa Reed for your honest assessment of where my original project was going. Without your butt kicking this book would not have happened as quickly.

Jeff Ritzmann for designing the cover at the drop of a hat. Many people claim they'd do anything for a friend. You actually do! You're the best friend I could ask for.

Mary Vaeni for editing a good chunk of this and all of your support. I deeply appreciate how you selflessly give to help your son even if you don't quite know what to make of me. *That's* a mother!

Thank you all. I love you.

This book is dedicated to all of the indigenous peoples of the world who carry out Original Instruction while we kill you to build one giant conformist amusement park. Singularity, indeed.

This book is dedicated to Peter Kingsley who gets it and speaks it eloquently. Thanks for keeping the lights on.

- And -

This book is dedicated to *Her*.

FOREWORD

Let me say straight out the gate that this book is like nothing I've read before. It's a brilliant dissection of obviously real and profound personal experiences of the author and a detailed questioning of what happened and what they meant. His bizarre experiences could easily have taken him where it has taken many before him, into established pigeonholes each judged with tags like UFO Abductee, Channeller, Hoaxer—or if one does not align with what he says, delusional.

Jeremy Vaeni is an intelligent man and a deep thinker who has been as honest with his many experiences as anyone I've known. At the beginning of the book he sets about encouraging, even prodding the reader to open up to his experiment, the experiment being to view just about everything you have read before about the paranormal and consciousness *differently*, very differently. For example he suggests that, whatever you have been told by the well-known gurus about becoming fully enlightened, it's not possible because one is never actually fully enlightened until death.

I have also had a series of inexplicable experiences myself since first becoming heavily involved in paranormal and consciousness research almost 30 years ago and traveling the world extensively. So when I read the various accounts of things that he claims happened to him, I know them to be true. I find his openness and questioning of those events extremely refreshing and brave.

His questioning of what *real* is, in its fullest and most complete sense, and *who or what* is behind these happenings along with *what they mean*, is at the center of the book. Is there a message from someone somewhere unseen? Is all of this some kind of reflection of a part of ourselves? The author, through honest and meticulous intellectual research, has discovered there is an URGENCY to all this.

I believe that this book has likely been partly written, not coincidentally, by unseen entities for the extraordinary transition in which humanity is now involved. Multiplexed changes that are taking place now on a huge scale are not necessarily going to be pleasant. But the reading of this book will be invaluable for us all as we try to understand the new world we are entering, who we are, and what we have to learn. As the world changes so do we.

Last but not least, the book is brilliantly written with Jeremy Vaeni's great sense of humor allowing the personable man that he is to treat the reader as a friend. The humor is not just fun and appealing, but it also is an important ingredient in what at times could be intellectually challenging for some readers unfamiliar with the subjects covered—I mean challenging in a healthy sense because his thinking is new. Not everyone will agree with his conclusions or how he reached them. Most, though, will see the merits of his approach.

His conclusions are powerful and I support them strongly. What I know as surely as I can is that, if we don't wake up soon, we and the many species for which we must assume guardianship will die—hence the URGENCY to Jeremy Vaeni's journey and all of ours.

Colin Andrews
Engineer, Int'l Human Consciousness Researcher & Author
January 24, 2011

PREFACE

If I tell you that all things manifest inside of a formless intelligence called *nothingness*, does that have any meaning for you? How about if I say that this intelligence is alive, so even though all of the things in it have separate identities, they are nonetheless transcended and included within the singular identity of nothingness? If it's true that all things exist as separate entities within one entity, then separation is an illusion. A functional illusion, but an illusion nonetheless.

Formless intelli-wah? Functional who with the what now? I know this is dense reading for a preface but bear with me.

What if I went on to say that you and I are a couple of the things manifesting within formless intelligence that can directly connect with it when we are as still as nothingness? If I tell you that this is the goal of meditation, does that have meaning for you?

Let me clarify: meditation doesn't mean *you* are still; it's the brain that must be still. You can't be still because you are activity. That's your nature. In fact, you're the thing that has to die for stillness to be the case.

Yup, it's an unfortunate fact that your brain has to kill you as its driving force for the self-aware aspect of formless intelligence to become its driving force.

Think of it this way: If you strip away all physical things there is nothing. When the brain strips away all mental things there is nothing. Nothingness is indivisible; we're talking about the same nothingness in both instances and this nothingness is alive. It is consciousness.

Consciousness isn't just some inert thing floating around; it is intelligence and so it's active. In physics we call this activity *force*. Force is what makes energy form waves and particles and gives them their instruction. Any physicist who wants to keep her job will not tell you that force is consciousness, even if she believes it. She'll say, "Force just is." To go further is to evoke the word *God* and that's where religions rear their ugly heads to misinform you on what *God* means.

So, force just is. That's where mainstream science stands on the matter and unwittingly they are correct. All things just are because all things are manifestations of formless intelligence.

That's physics. For people, force manifests a different kind of instruction called *Truth*. Truth with a capital "T" because it's not relative. There are relative truths to be sure, but much to the chagrin of postmodern philosophers, there's also absolute Truth. Absolute Truth is the force that takes shape most obviously as insights into the human condition and the nature of reality. They come clearly when the brain meditates.

There's a lot more to it than this but let's keep it simple for now: force in physics is instruction; force in meditation is instruction. Think about what that means. It means that there is instruction in you right now waiting for the brain to shut up so it can be heard.

We have a word for brains that assume Truth's identity: *enlightened*. You may wonder why multitudes of self-help and self-empowerment books geared toward enlightening you exist if Truth is this elegant. Why the classes and texts on meditation? Enlightenment can't really be this simple can it? These sound like fair questions until you reverse them: We've had thousands of years to get this right; if any of these time-consuming systems work, then why do new ones keep popping up? Why isn't everyone enlightened already?

Here's why systems fail: When the brain assumes the enlightened state of no-self, understanding and instruction pour in. If you've experienced this, as I have, it's easy to believe that you can share these epiphanies with others to help wake them up. Unfortunately, you cannot because the insights came after the fact. First enlightenment, then deep insights. Why?—Because you, the seeker, must die for higher thought to be the case. You cannot know that which is beyond you. When the brain stops projecting you as its identity, that which was beyond becomes its identity.

God is the new you and you speak Truth. Sounds great if you ignore the pitfalls but think how many charlatans and delusional people through the ages have claimed to be God. You will do anything to remain as you are because fear of death is the ultimate driving force in our ordinary lives. You may not acknowledge this but it is. And so you will do anything not to die to enlightenment, including making up stories about an afterlife. Including saying you're already enlightened. And you may even convince yourself. In fact, you must. That is how the lie of you sustains itself.

Believe me, I'd love nothing more than to grow filthy rich from penning a middle-of-the-road tome full of platitudes and affirmations designed to validate your life and make you feel like you're on the right path. Self-empowerment books are a far easier sell than self-annihilation but it's time to get real about this. One is either enlightened or one is not. There is no overlooking that. Put another way, one is either asleep or awake.

Sleeping with one eye open means you're still half asleep. Truth is black and white on this issue. Simply knowing it means you've got one up on the spiritual gurus who write how-to books on achieving enlightenment. This raises a natural question: Why don't the one-eye opened spiritual leaders know they're still sleeping?

I'll see your pesky question and raise you another: How can they? They may see part of the room they're sleeping in but they're still caught up in the dream. They incorporate the room into the dream. The dream includes states and stages of consciousness that they climb and then drop a ladder down to you. This is a way one-eye-opened people delude themselves, for no matter how high they may have climbed on the spiritual ladder, they're on the ladder and the ladder breeds deception. Deception number one?—That there is a ladder at all.

What, none of you saw *The Matrix?*

Let's say that authentic spiritual gurus have more positive energy flowing through them informing their actions than average humans. We'll give them that. They are dreaming like the rest of us and in that dream they are beacons of light attracting dark creatures, namely us. Positive attracts negative like the workings of a cell. They want to enlighten followers, right? But how can they? They can only demonstrate what they themselves are, which is incomplete.

You ever read *The Power of Now*, by Eckhart Tolle? Please allow me to point out with zero arrogance in my heart precisely where he goes wrong. It is on page 6 of the first edition paperback. Soon after his enlightening epiphany Eckhart writes, "Before I knew it, I had an external identity again. I had become a spiritual teacher."[1]

Spiritual teacher? Uh-oh. That's code for "Move over, Deepak Chopra—There's a new positive reinforcer in town!"

Tolle's enlightenment experience is not in question. What's in question is what he did with it. He became a teacher.

Really, the first place he goes wrong is the book's subtitle, *A Guide To Spiritual Enlightenment*, but I was trying to be nice. There is no guidance, nothing to teach. There is if by enlightenment you mean moving to a different rung on the spiritual ladder, which is good for gaining some temporary inner peace. We aren't concerned with that definition. It's not good enough. There's always a high in the fantasy of climbing higher but once you're there, that which was higher becomes the floor. Eckhart Tolle, Deepak Chopra, and the rest of the New Age crowd teach you how to get high. That isn't enlightenment.

Just say no.

There are people like Jesus (assuming he said any of the *die into me* things attributed to him) and Adi Da,

---

[1] Tolle, Eckhart, *The Power of Now*, New World Library & Namaste Publishing, September 2004 edition, p.6.

who claimed they were God and that to live in relationship with them, even in their deaths, is to get as close to enlightenment as possible. Is there no truth to that? Or is there some *God on Earth* syndrome these people were afflicted with?

Who among us is not already God on Earth? Earth is God, wind, trees, this book and the hands that hold it, because matter is the thing side of No-Thing. Everything is God but not everything expresses God-self awareness. We can. We all can. And so there are not special people we must experience enlightenment vicariously through.

No-Thing, by the way, is a fancy-shmancy word for *God* that we'll discover in Chapter 1. For now, let's consider duality in terms of the alleged man-gods. Positive/negative duality is part of this dream we call *reality* so setting oneself up as a positive doorway through which the negative pass is delusional. If you want to call that a higher delusion, okay. In the realm of mental illness we'd say clinical depression is a lesser illness than schizophrenia. Both are afflictions; both cause suffering. The point is, leadership and authority are detrimental to spiritual awakening. Any meditation not born of you is a hand-me-down from one who has transcended where you are and is tossing you his old clothes. They may seem to fit or they may not. They are definitely not yours.

Take, for example, the classic instruction from Vietnamese Buddhist monk, Thich Nhat Hanh to do the dishes to do the dishes.[2] What a wonderful reminder to be in the moment. Problem is, he's the guy in the moment saying it because that's how guys in the moment think and you're the one interpreting it as a reminder to be what you're not: in the moment. For him it is a natural extension of himself to say such things. For you it creates friction because you want to be that and aren't. The reminder reminds you to repress the

---

[2] Actually, it's "Washing the dishes to wash the dishes." Nhat Hanh, Thich, *The Miracle of Mindfulness*, Beacon Press, 1987 edition, p.3.

frantic creature of time that you are and pay attention to the now as an exercise.

When an enlightened one (or nearly enlightened one) tells you to "do this to achieve that" or "pay total attention to what you're doing moment to moment" where Spirit is concerned it can never be true for you. True for them, not true for you. For you it becomes dull, meaningless routine even if you started off strong.

One who thinks rightly cannot teach another to do the same because any of their "lessons" are born of the enlightened brain, which became enlightened the moment it stopped thinking (killed its personal self) only to resurrect as a totally new thinker in formless self. The teachings don't apply except as a means to keep you as tranquil and peaceful as possible while you carry on this unenlightened life. The assumption that you will not transcend is not cynical, by the way, it's statistical.

***

We all secretly long for an intervention that will sustain us but there is only Love, which burns through us when the brain allows. Love is the passion that drives Truth. From Love springs creation with its surfaces, charges, dualities and so forth. All things must be expressed, including suffering. However, Love says you don't have to be the one expressing it. Love gives you the option, the free will choice. Love doesn't force you to come home but leaves the door wide open.

Love is not something found in a sermon, a guidance, a teaching, or even this book. Love just is. And when you just are, you are Love. That's not poetic license, that's a fact.

INTRODUCTION

It's not as if I wanted to write a book antithetical to everything we hold true any more than you're going to want to read it, but here's what happened: In 2003 I published a quiet book with a loud title, *I Know Why The Aliens Don't Land!*, and have ever since been writing its sequel. In my head the sequel was a beautiful thing: more misogynistic humor, more self-deprecation, more about my not-so-alien abductions (don't ask), and then, in the end, more literary devices employed to awaken you to a new meaning of what it is to be human.

Right. Like that ever works.

I was putting the finishing touches on that book when a friend read it and said what I already knew in my heart, if not my brain: My story is irrelevant and we don't have time to dillydally. Since the crux of my nonfiction work is about humanity transcending its current definition of itself, write that book, already. Stop tiptoeing around the issue. Give baby his medicine.

Waking up, transcending all that we know, is serious business—so serious that you must bring your sense of humor with you or you will never make it. However, the type of humor I employ in my work is not always born of this truth but of trying to identify with my cynical generation (Gen-Xer here) who laugh at everything as a means to remain inert. Problem is, they'd laugh off the topics at hand before they'd ever read my books and so the author has no audience. Such is the drawback of cynicism.

I was going to call the sequel *The Skeleton Key To All Worlds* because it's my experience that we contain a piece of biology undiscovered by science in or around the lower spine that opens like a gill and connects us to unbridled consciousness. If that sounds like a woo-woo

New Age theory now, just ye wait. We are going to flesh it out in a rational way.

Incidentally, I've been known to attack the falsehoods of New Age and mainstream religion alike, so this book is an ironic undertaking. My beef with them is that I am a product of the post-self enlightenment process this book speaks to and so I know it's real. I have no choice but to know that and it's nearly impossible to hold a reasonable conversation about it using the terminology they have bastardized without you reflexively thinking back to them, rolling your eyes, and groaning. Or worse, *embracing*, which makes me groan.

The difference between what I'm going to share with you and the material I rail against is that New Age and religious dogma often lack or bury rational components. Truth always contains a rational component because it is holistic. There are paradoxes to be sure but they must make sense.

New Age can mean anything. It's set up to say "anything is possible." Under that guise a New Age author can pen any claim and say, "Just believe me." While it is true that anything is possible it is not true that anything is probable or actual. So anything is possible in the virtual storage unit called *imagination* but not everything can exist outside of it. And religions are so problematic with their political and cultural overlay that it's self-evident. I need not bother saying more than that. Still, you probably found this in the New Age section of your bookstore. Is that irony or a paradox?

***

Normally, those who buy books with words like *god, truth, enlightenment, transcendence* and *self* in them do so in anticipation that the texts will confirm their belief systems or provide a new one. Truth is not served well by belief or disbelief, so I will now tear those systems down while stealing back the language abused by all religious movements, thank you very much. But what I won't do is preface everything with the experiences that "qualify" me to detonate bombs and talk about this stuff in the first place. That would set me up as the object you get to judge and make a guru or a liar of.

Again: no time to dillydally.

Frankly, it doesn't matter if I work at a monastery or at a Chuck E. Cheese; it doesn't matter if I write books about being an alien abductee from my apartment or from my padded cell. These words on Spirit and the human condition are either true or they are not. They are broader, richer, deeper, purer than what you live by or they are not. Even so, they are completely useless beyond a certain point. Whether you get to that point, build another house on it and live there, I cannot control. It sure would be sweet if you didn't.

So, here we go. My little attempt at answering everything so that your brain has nowhere left to run.

In Act I, I spoon feed the answers to every previously unanswerable (or poorly articulated) major question about us I can think of. I don't do this to start a new religion or cult of me. I do it to box in your seeking, searching brain.

The brain is like a detective always asking why and how things are the way they are. Unlike a detective, who presumably really does want answers, the brain seeks to deceive, not answer, itself. Denying its true nature is the game your brain is playing right now. Playing it with you as the pawn. That game ends here.

Act II is where the experiment really kicks in. Oh, did I mention this is an experiment? Yeah. Read it at your own risk. Act I speaks to you, the reader, but Act II speaks directly to the brain that projects you. If all goes well you will be dead by the end of it. Don't worry. It's for the best.

Trust me, I'm a stranger.

Finally, Act III is... well... there is no Act III. I call what would be Act III *No Act*. It's time for the veils to fall and the acting to stop. It's time to understand why we called ourselves human beings in the first place. Everything we need to be whole is hidden in plain sight.

Not by secret societies. Not by brilliant artists. By us. All of us.

We are our best-kept secret.

***

There is a theme to this book, a mantra of sorts, which I touched on in the Preface: One eye open is still half asleep.

On our best day that is how we live. That describes the typical enlightened person: awake-ish but still attached to the dream. How can the Dalai Lama be a fully integrated human and still be Buddhist? It's impossible unless he's still Buddhist simply because, Hey! You've gotta be something! Doesn't matter what as long as you do it impeccably.

But that's not what's going on. He still writes books promoting Buddhist paths and ways that he would like you to follow. He preaches about nonattachment while remaining attached to Buddhism. Conflict of interest, much?

Enlightenment is what happens when the self dissolves completely. The self. *You.* You are not real. You are a projection of the brain. When the brain stops projecting you universal energy, often called kundalini, chi, or n/om comes alive in the body. (For the sake of brevity, let's stick with kundalini.) It informs the body with its own will. This will is the healing force of Truth.

Think of kundalini as an operating system running parallel to your own will. This system is all about health. To that end it makes the body perform yoga, acupressure, and other physically healthy acts. That's right, an energy comes alive in the body and moves it around when you step aside. It won't make you do The Robot but it might have you do Tai Chi. Equally embarrassing.

If this notion sounds foreign to you, it probably is. *Kriya (pronounced kree*yah)* is the Sanskrit word for these spontaneous movements. We don't have a word for it in English. A priest might wrongly call it demon possession. A psychiatrist might classify such performances as a neurological disorder. Also wrong. This is one of those rare times when something walks and quacks like a duck but isn't.

Kundalini also awakens psychic centers in the body that biologists have yet to discover. It floods the brain with logical insights into the human condition not unlike the ones you're about to read. If you don't try to reassert your own will over the process, kundalini will undo the damage you've unwittingly caused to the body. All of this is to shape up the organic vessel for the big enchilada: God-self identity.

Since the brain stopping its normal activity of projecting you is the trigger that activates kundalini, paths to enlightenment are useless. They are the things we tell ourselves we're on to never actually get there. What path can get you over yourself? Any direction you choose you're the director. Any path you take, it's your self-fulfilled prophecy waiting for you at the finish line.

While it is a fact that in the current scheme of how we live and define *human nature* it's healthier to take a holistic approach, discipline yourself, love your neighbor, and all that fine stuff, this book maintains that that's not what humans are for. That's not our purpose. Trying to be good and caring people is still avoiding the issue.

The issue is, are we God-alive or not? What does that even mean? Maybe you've heard the term *God-alive* before. Perhaps you think God is a father in the sky or a mother of the earth, or some energy you tap into to create your own reality. The world according to you. Yikes.

Possibly you don't believe in God at all. God is a concept used to oppress people and explain things irrationally, a holdover from the time before philosophy and science choked the mystery out of everything. For you, God-alive probably means the self-actualized state psychologists go on about, nothing more. *Booooriiiiing.*

The thing the believer and disbeliever have in common is belief. You both believe you have an answer and it is based in thought. The believer adopts cultural thought constructs and runs with 'em while the disbeliever sees the folly in that and sticks to the material and theoretical sciences. It is a smart move not to believe in beliefs but surely it's the cliff-dive of hypocrisy to then slap another definition onto the unknowable by saying there's no such thing.

You cannot know the unknowable. You cannot deny the unknowable. You cannot even approach the unknowable, for you are a thought construct born of the brain. You do not exist but in your head. Deep down you know this but you suppress it. It's top secret.

You hide Truth even from yourself and in that way do you set yourself up as God, as the center from which reality manifests. It's no wonder, then, that in America, at least, corporate advertising has trended toward campaigns and products containing the words *I, My, You, Smart*. Businesses don't do that blindly or at the behest of evil overlords from a shadow government. They do it because that's what the common folk they interview and analyze in focus groups say they want to own—not just products but products they feel are extensions of their own awesome selves.

Now here's the part where I try a scare tactic to get you to feel urgency for waking up. I could have chosen global warming and the imminent collapse of our livable environment, but that's *so* 2006. Plus, you might be one of those holdouts who believe the corporate shills paid to tell you that global warming is not happening or we need more data, yada-yada, so I'm going to go another inevitable-outcome-of-our-actions route and scare you with the lesser vilified fact that we are turning ourselves into... *MEATBOTS!*

That's right, folks. We're going cyborg before our very eyes. We used to care about this back in the warning phase when science fiction authors wrote about barcodes on our foreheads and transistors in our teeth, but once we started going cyborg for real, we couldn't have been less disturbed. In fact, we welcomed it.

It all started with a nasty little addiction to television. Animals love shiny objects and we're no different. This shiny object is the ultimate. It speaks our language and shows us things, imagines for us, and tells us how to feel. But that's not enough for us, is it?

We don't want to just watch television anymore. We're not even satisfied with being on television anymore. We want to *be* television. We went from spectator (watching shows) to participant (being guests on talk shows) to being the show itself (reality television.) Now we're at the point where even that's not enough. We have to have other information scrolling on the TV screen unrelated to the show we're watching and we are often instructed to run to our computers and telephones to interact with the show.

Without getting too paranoid here, what do you think the final result of that evolution will be? What self-fulfilling prophecy awaits us at the end?

It's as if we took the warnings and the fears and the projections of sci fi writers from yesteryear and said, "Cool. I'll be a cyborg. If getting the iThink chip planted in my brain means I never have to fish my purse for a credit card again, consider me sold."

Imagine a world where people are implanted with computer chips for commercial purposes and one day a virus hits that allows its creator to assume control of the population. One dictator in many bodies. If I'd written this even ten years ago you might have laughed and called me nuts, but the sad fact is you can imagine this as a legitimate possibility now.

And where does this impulse stem from? This impulse to cram as much information into our noggins as possible and push toward oneness via technological interconnectivity?

It stems from the repression of the God-alive self for the sake of the brain-derived self. That, not technology per se, is the root of the problem.

How this predicament came about is natural. Nobody is at fault. We'll get to that, no worries, and we'll do so because what was natural then is unnatural now. Now is the moment to transcend all of this nonsense we wrongly ascribe to human nature.

How do we do that, you ask? We don't, for there is no *how*. A *how* implies you doing something and you is the thing that must dissolve. Oh, this ain't gonna be pretty, folks. You have to die for this. Die while the body is alive.

With you out of the way God-self has room to maneuver.

Is that what you want? Of course not. You want to live. You may say otherwise but at the moment of Truth you buckle. You've always buckled since the beginning of us.

Here's an analogy for what I'm driving at that works: You ever see that movie *The Abyss* where the people have to wear liquid oxygen masks? If not, just imagine that your head is trapped in a helmet filled with liquid and you're told that you have to breathe. That's the death of you, right?—because you'll drown. Except you won't. You will breathe. If only we as a species could apply that analogy to our sense of self this whole miserable game would be over and we'd move on.

But nooooo-ooooo! You wanna hold your breath and live in fear of release. You want to build belief systems around physical release and suppress, suppress, suppress what you are right now in the flesh. What are you? What is this thing we cannot define, this unknowable we cannot drag into the world of knowns?

Lean in. I'm about to whisper the tiniest of secrets. Don't tell anyone you wouldn't want to annihilate by sharing with them. And if in the course of reading this you feel like you're being annihilated, put the book down and let that happen. You will have gotten your money's worth.

ACT I

**IS-NESS IS COMPRISED OF WHAT ISN'T.
NOW IS TIMELESS TIME.
NONSENSICAL RIDDLES CREATE SENSE.
NO WONDER SAGES HIDE BEHIND BEARDS.**

CHAPTER 1
No-Thing

In the beginning... there was no beginning. There was no ending. There was no *was* and no *will be*. Why do I feel like that should sound catchier?—There's gotta be a better way to write that! Either way it's a fact of existence: There is no beginning and there is no end. There is only Truth, only God. These are synonymous terms and have no relationship to the dogmas we've concocted about them. Is it possible to dust them off and use them even though they've been sitting on everyone's mental shelves for eons?

As noted, religious and New Age "spiritual" folk have hijacked this terminology for their own gain. Let's steal it back. Let's use the common language but throw out all definitions and start anew. Let's see what happens. In fact, let's not rest there; let us figure out why these belief systems exist and utilize such terms with authority in the first place.

It's all coming, baby. The big reveal. With nothing up my sleeve, *Presto!* First, let's talk about time and intelligence.

How We Experience Time

Because we're trapped in time, we tend to think either linearly or cyclically. Linear thinkers view history as a straight line from the past to the present and presume a future. If nature or nukes or asteroids or aliens don't kill us off we will evolve and evolve and evolve forever.

Cyclical thinkers say that history repeats itself in giant loops that spiral out. In each loop humanity has a chance to transcend to a higher stage of being, however one defines it. Failing that, as we're prone to do, natural catastrophes kick in like clockwork wiping out the societies and advances we've made and we have to start over from scratch. Why no one has made a video game about this yet is beyond me.

Cyclical time is a linear unfolding. People who exclusively believe in linear time often say, "History repeats itself," but people who believe in cyclical time really, really mean it. It's the difference between drawing a straight line with a ruler and superimposing a spiral over that line. Both of those are correct to an extent but there's something even more fundamentally correct and it is this: Time is an illusion.

You've heard that bandied about right? And Einstein proved it in a way that doesn't apply to our day-to-day lives. That's cute but useless. Thanks, Einstein.

How can we prove that time is an illusion in practical terms? How can we see it? Why does it have that ring of truth to some but get shrugged off by others? What's missing from that declaration, *Time is an illusion?*

Travel back with me, won't you? Back before people. Back before dinosaurs. Back before planets and stars. Back before matter. Back before the Big Bang banged big.

How far back dare we travel?—All the way back to nothing.

Nothingness Equals Formless Intelligence

It seems that nothing is the case prior to all things. Fair enough, right? Take away everything and there's nothing. The problem is, nothing isn't just nothing; it's also a thing. That's what the kids call a paradox.

What kind of a thing is nothing you ask? Good question. It's a concept.

All concepts exist in intelligence. We tend to think intelligence exists in the brain—and that's true—but here we have a concept that can only exist when the brain does not. Therefore it follows that this *nothing* is intelligence itself.

Are you seeing this?

Nothing is the only concept around that does not exist as a product of a thinking brain. It is a concept that seems to prove intelligence exists prior to the brain, prior to all things including time.

When we say *intelligence* we're not talking about the intellect alone. We're talking about the ultimate consciousness that contains intellect as a quality. So, what is this intelligence of which I speak? Well, we know the word implies action. Intelligence is no mere thing, no lifeless object sitting around. It's alive, it's aware, it's active—and this alive, aware, active intelligence that seems to exist prior to the universe is, by definition, formless.

Scrape away all things and we are left with this active, formless intelligence. What is its action? Its action is creation of all the things we just scraped away. If you want to get cute you could say that this fact is contained in the very composition of the word *nothing* because *no* comes first, followed by *thing*. Add a hyphen and you see it: No-Thing.

No is formlessness and *thing* is form. Formlessness and form are married in the simple word, *nothing.*

No creates *thing*, or so it seems. It seems that we've proven there is a formless intelligence creating form, but look closely at that word *nothing* one more time. Yes, *thing* falls after *no* in the word but the word itself is one movement. One word, not two. No division.

There is no division between formless intelligence and form. I created the division by saying "Let's go back to the time before time," because that's easier to comprehend. We're linear people so it's easier to wrap our heads around linear suppositions, but this ultimate intelligence we're talking about does not exist prior to all things. It exists prior to *and inclusive of* all things. That is an important distinction.

Nothingness exists prior to and inclusive of thingness. In other words, formless intelligence transcends and includes everything. Therefore, the question of what this intelligence is creating is a wrong question because there isn't a creator separate from its creation. There is only the action of creation itself.

That in its totality is God.

This is bad news for the various religions that want you to believe there is a God separate from you, an intelligent designer that watches over you, guides you, judges you, and so forth. This is also bad news for the materialists and reductionists who believe that every real thing will be discovered with tools of reason. They have all just been proven wrong. Ouch.

What are we up to Chapter 2 and we've already proven God? I'd say we're making pretty good time, wouldn't you?

Alright, breathe. There's more.

CHAPTER 2
Why There Is Death

So, we've discovered that there is formless intelligence prior to and inclusive of all forms. We're calling this intelligence *God* to steal that term back from the religious hijackers. Because all things exist in God there is no time. From God's self-aware perspective there is only now, only is-ness, only being in which everything manifests.

God Is What God Is Doing

God is being. Be-ing. God's state is God's action. Put differently, God is the ultimate state of imagining. If you want to say, "God is the imagining of everything" to imply that all energy, matter, and action exist within that imagining, fine. I won't stop you. Just don't get confused and say, "There is a God doing the imagining" as if that action produces something outside itself.

Again, there is no God divided from the imagining, no actor divided from the act. There is only imagining, only acting. This is because God is not an entity separate from being. God is being itself. (And no-being its non-self, but let's not confuse the point any further.)

So, it's like you've got this bodiless, formless intelligence that just is. And that intelligence—in simply being—is radiating energy that manifests the universe like a heat mirage from pavement. Life, death, time, measurement, separation, matter—these are all aspects of the mirage found in the Thing part of No-Thing.

A fancier term for that mirage is *necessary illusion*. *Necessary* means it can be no other way. Nothingness cannot divide into more nothingness. However, all things must be expressed so our ultimate intelligence here must create the necessary illusion of divisions within itself, which is where space and time come in.

Let us say that timelessness and formless intelligence are qualities of No-Thing contained in the No aspect. They will not exist in the physical universe because the physical universe is not comprised of those qualities. Those qualities are not things one can comprise, they just are. And as we agreed that which cannot be comprised cannot be divided.

In other words, nothingness has its qualities that can't be recreated, but its action is creation. What is it creating?—Forms. And with forms come time. And with time comes lifespan.

Don't Fear The Reaper

It's okay if you're confused. Let's refine this:

Formless/timeless intelligence is alive. It *is* consciousness. That consciousness is forever creating everything. Everything exists in time and therefore has lifespan. Organisms die and matter disintegrates because that which is being created must be different than formlessness and timelessness.

What's different from timelessness?—Time.

What's different from formlessness?—Form.

What's different from life?—Death.

Can we have just life?—No. If life existed without death there would be no room to move. Eventually there would be no space between objects and everything would smother itself in one giant eternal ball of inert hell. Imagine being trapped in a sardine can forever. Yuck. Thank God for death.

Can we have just death?—No. Just death would immediately bring us out of creation and back to nothingness.

So we see that what is different from life—and is necessarily the case—is not just death but death within life. The cycle has to exist even though it's an illusion.

Do you need a minute to process this? Take a break. I'll see you next chapter.

CHAPTER 3
What Free Will Is

Aaaaaand back. Feel better? It's a lot of words, right? And sometimes ya just have to sit with them for them to mean something. Sit with this:

We said that the Thing aspect of No-Thing is matter. But it is more than that. Matter isn't just particles and rocks and stuff; it's also organisms. It's life. It's the full expression of timeless/formless intelligence played out in time and form.

Once you have time you have divisions and measurements. This is as true for material things as it is for immaterial things such as intelligence. To that end earth has insect intelligence, animal intelligence, plant, human and so on, each with its own subdivisions. All of these creatures, if they do not live their full potential, mutate or die out.

Humans, unlike the other creatures, are at a disadvantage when it comes to this "mutate or die" principle because we've transcended instinct. It's harder for a human to be a human than, say, an insect an insect, because we are less mechanical. We have choice.

Other beings make choices too, but not the ultimate one we can make. Not the one that separates us from them. An ant is always being an ant living out the ant's full potential. If there is a mutation that needs to occur for ants to survive it will happen, as it must, without ant consent. This goes for all life forms on up the food chain until you hit humans. Ours is the only species not living in its full potential.

Only Human After All

Most people assume humans are being human by exercising free will. As usual, most people are wrong. For... let's see—by my watch—millennia now, we've wrongly defined free will as the ability to choose one's actions.

What's wrong with that? The plural part. There is only one free will choice you can ever make from which all others branch and it is this: To live the point of view of self or to live the point of view of God. Put another way, to live separation or to live oneness. Put yet a third way, to live the point of view of thingness or to live the point of view of nothingness.

Nothingness is whole and thingness partial.

If that makes sense to you, then you might rightly ask how it is we can live the point of view of nothingness when we are things, organisms. The answer is that the body is already thingness. It already represents that point of view and so there is no need for our consciousness to also represent it. We are a redundant species like no other on earth.

Animals already represent animal consciousness. Some animals are self-aware. Some may even make choices beyond their instinctual boundaries but they always snap back into instinct's lockstep for they are restricted by its overriding command. We have a much richer psychology than animals but more than that we have the ability to be God-self aware.

All things must be expressed because all things are the result of formless intelligence creating its self. Another way to say it is that the totality of consciousness must divide itself within itself. Those divisions—those forms—are embedded in formless intelligence. This has to be. No choice. God has no free will choice on this issue.

However, free will must be expressed because... well... all things must! God expresses free will through some of the things choicelessly being created. Since those things are also aspects of God (remember, there's no division between creator/creation—that is the only division that cannot exist), this ultimate intelligence is experiencing free will through organisms. If all universes are God's body, then all the expressions therein are God's body parts. Humans are a part of the body that can express God's self-awareness. When the brain abandons its own point of view, God's perspective becomes the case.

Cool.

***

All types of organisms come equipped with a unique spin on self-awareness. Ours is that when we dissolve the self-awareness of the brain, God-self awareness takes over. Why?—because all things must be expressed. That phrase again. All things must be expressed including the undivided self-awareness of God through its creation.

One could say that animals being animal means animals being self-aware. Humans being human means humans being God-self aware. But no one I know is. Do you know anyone God-self aware? Doesn't everyone pretty much think that being human means being self-aware like animals but with novelty add-ons such as a grasp on complex symbols so that when we screw up we say something idiotic like, "That's just human nature?"

What do you think happens when a species doesn't realize its potential? If the butterfly never leaves the cocoon, what results?

We need to abandon brain-based intelligence so that formless intelligence may come alive in its own creation—us! Why don't we know this about ourselves? Why do we relegate such a change to saviors, Buddhas, or the impossible? Why isn't this the thrust of our lives?

Unconsciously it is the thrust. We may have insulated ourselves from Truth's song but at the deepest layer of us the song plays faintly and beautifully. The beat of it antagonizes the insulation; the vibration escapes it and motivates us like a dissonant memory of what we are nagging us to wake up from our perpetual fugue state.

Still, how did we come to embody this dilemma in the first place?

CHAPTER 4
The Story of Us

All things must be expressed including this dilemma we find ourselves in. Gee, maybe I should have made "All things must be expressed" the mantra for this book instead of "One eye open is still half asleep." Eh. No time for regrets. Forge on, explorers! We must discover the mechanics behind our disconnect because even though all things must be expressed we don't have to express our mistakes forever.

Fear Of The Newborn

Let's time travel again, this time away from nothingness, away from the primordial ooze of creation. Let's fast forward to the instance when humankind stepped out of its animal clothes and into something else. Let's go to the moment after we woke up.

We're not concerned with how this happened. We don't know how and it's not integral to enlightenment that we figure it out. Why it happened is that it inevitably must and that fact will reveal itself through the book. For now, let's concern ourselves with what happened next. What happened has never been explained before this writing. That kind of historical precedence is what a salesman might call "added value."

Here now is your added value. Here is the story of us....

One day an ape-like animal woke up into a new sense of reality and experienced awareness on a level the species had never known. Its reflexive response to this was fear: the terror of the newborn.

The animal—call it a human—saw separation between the world and itself in a radically different way. Its comprehension of growth and death was likewise revolutionary. The brain of the human responded to its terror by immediately splitting its new awareness in two: conscious and unconscious.

Everything the creature just was repressed into a rich psychological stew smothered by shock and fear. This we call the unconscious mind.

The human's new individuated self-identity was a shallow mask of a thing, an orderly defense mechanism that repressed the unconscious. This persona is what we call the conscious mind.

That's all psychology 101 material, right? But here's the part that's never been said. Keep in mind this is all instantaneous....

The conscious mask, the persona, having no other guide, initially formed itself by mimicking the orderliness of the brain cells projecting it. Essentially, the new human woke out of instinct only to mimic instinct. One could say the self-aware brain turned its sight on its own functioning for parenting. What the brain taught its newborn ego was this: Act in patterns and try to make sense of the world, for just as my cells work mechanically and repetitively so shall you.

And why not? Pattern works for the brain, why shouldn't it work for the brain-projected self? It was only logical that the brain of the human animal woke up, immediately self-reflected, and then sent instruction to its newly formed ego telling it to act in patterns just like it (the brain) does.

The ego didn't stop there. It had a broad external world to explore and endure so it further developed its boundaries via information received through the physical senses and on its intuited understanding of nature. It was now free to use the survival tools of instinct for its own personal fortification. All of that is why people to this day seek patterns, live in patterns, form relationships in patterns, and so on.

Transcend And Include

The ego didn't limit itself to external exploration; it explored its interior domain as well. The interior was trickier because it contained no substance, no tangible boundary and yet there were all these concepts and impulses lurking about. Shapes and math. Ewe, math. And as always there was Truth pulsating in the background trying to get in.

Some things in headspace floated around independently but most were co-created by the ego as it built up its sense of self and engaged the symbols and feelings waiting there. Ego's approach was the tried and true mimicking of principles it observed in the external world. Chief among them was one of the basic organizing principles appearing in nature called *transcend and include.* In physics the atom transcends and includes the electron, the molecule transcends and includes both, and the cell transcends and includes all three within it. Ecosystems work the same way. We call it the food chain.

There's a term for things that practice the transcend and include principle: *holon.* It means a part that contains a whole system that is itself part of another whole system.

Integral philosopher Ken Wilber says there is a legitimate *transcend and include* spiritual rising that occurs through states and stages of consciousness. He calls it "the secret impulse of evolution."[3] He means that Spirit descends into matter and forgets itself in its creation only to rise back to full awareness as a game it delights in. We've certainly set up that obstacle course, but from the ultimate perspective there is no Spirit descending, forgetting, and ascending for miserable fun. The ultimate transcends and includes that journey. We've been able to access the ultimate from day one, we just never did. The trump card was in our hand the whole time but we feared playing it. Therefore, spiritually speaking, there is only one transcendental

---

[3] Wilber, Ken, *A Brief History of Everything*, Shambhala Publications, Inc., 2000 edition, p.44.

move and that's from brain-self to God-self awareness. The moves in between are our own and don't actually lead there.

The Psycho-spiritual Ladder Is Monkey Bars

Wilber and his peers describe the climbing games that we play very well. He has eloquently mapped them out in his work. Unfortunately, that and a nickel will not buy you a cup of coffee let alone wake you up. Swinging from the highest rung of alleged spiritual development is still playing in illusion.

From a subjective rung on the ladder there is up, down, and where you are. Objectively, the ladder has no fixed position. It is just as horizontal as it is vertical. You might as well be swinging on monkey bars, so why the serious face?

Men and women of any and all persuasions may at a given moment wakeup to their God-ness, be they fundamentalist, yogi, monk, tribesman, business woman, materialist, or alchemist, because Truth has no chain of being, no ladder of ascension. There are no steps toward Truth, only the one free will choice to step away from it.

It bears repeating: Physically, in nature, there is this chain of being comprised of holons. Spiritually, the chain does not exist. We live like it exists but it is actually an invention of the human brain that converted the details of physical nature into multi-tiered personal and then consensus reality long ago.

There is only separation/oneness, or dualism/non-dualism if you like. There is no such thing as *more* separation, *more* dualism. Those seemingly authentic further links creating a chain are not real. This is what we mean when we say humans only have one free will choice: to live God-self or to live brain-self.

The former is the real ever-present case. God.

The latter is an invention of the brain that internalized its exterior observations long, long ago. You.

Ne'er the twain shall meet.

And Now Back To Our Story

So with Truth blocked out, consciousness divided, and a mechanical framework for interacting with the world in place, the brain-born self felt comfortable enough, familiar enough in its own skin to face the world.

How did the new human ego face the world? Ah. Good question. It set itself up as the center of everything and moved from there. It interacted with the world from three perspectives familiar to us as literary devices: 1st-person, 2nd-person, 3rd-person. On this Wilber and I agree and I steal. These perspectives translate as I, we, it. Technically, 2nd-person is *you* but there is no such thing as you. There is only how two or more I's relate. Therefore, 2nd-person perspective is relationship.

Simply put, the new human's interaction with the world was (and remains) this: I observe something, I talk it over with you or relate directly to it, and in so doing I identify it (or more uncommonly I identify *as* it.)

With these perspectives we come to know and understand and categorize unknowns, which temporarily alleviates our fears. There's just one problem: Beyond the known and the unknown there is the unknowable. Humans do not recognize the unknowable. We collapse it into the unknown and the known.

The tools we use to collapse it have evolved recently from religion to science. If the delusion of religion is to say, "I know the unknowable," then science is the deluded thing that says, "Religion doesn't know but I'm going to find out."

Religion denies the unknown and the unknowable by irrationally claiming to know everything. Science sees through that enough to recognize unknowns yet remains in denial of the unknowable. Science collapses the unknowable into the unknown (future discoveries.) Religion collapses all of that into the known (creation myths.)

In either case the quest for knowledge is the quest for self-fortification. We don't want Truth. We want certainty. That is what we seek. That is why most of our interactions with each other involve trying to win over the other to our point of view.

You need to see things my way. Walk a mile in my shoes. I know how to run things. I know why so-and-so is an idiot. I think God is this because that's what makes sense to me. Me-me-me. Or if you're more timid that that, you join a collective. Us-us-us. I'm right. We're right. That makes you wrong. I'll fight you or tolerate you. I am the center of everything because I'm so very afraid that I'm not.

Memory And The Mortal Self Center

What a denial we live in, eh? Fearing death, blocking out Truth, manipulating normal drives to aid in blocking out Truth, calling our mistakes human nature... the list goes on. We're busy people and we're not even real! We're just some holograms our brains project so they can feel like they're immortal and evolving until Alzheimer's or death. Still, that doesn't keep us from our hectic schedules and the diseased relationships we consider normal.

Why is it so hard to maintain healthy relationships when we're all in this together?—Because the thing we're all in together isn't just life, it's also delusion. We're all in this delusion together and so we're behaving accordingly.

The moment animal instinct is set free, the brain, in its death fear, snatches it and perverts its workings for ego preservation. The reflexive action and inherited instruction of the animal get sent to the human body shop for detailing. The body has a life drive and now that drive extends into this new holographic mental unreality where each fear gets named and personified along with its opposite, the "cure" or "god" or "spirit" we call upon in our times of unbearable trouble. I'm getting ahead of myself. Let's stick to the body.

The body does not want to die. It isn't immortal so it projects a self that it feels is immortal. To aid in the delusion it perverts the rightful use of a little tool you may have heard of called *memory*. Memory reminds you what to do and what not to do, where to go and where to stay away from, and what time *The Simpsons* is on.

Since the new standard model human has more mental freedom than his animal predecessor he can do more with memory. He can allocate some of its use to areas where it doesn't belong such as personal relationship. And because he can he does, for the brain needs all the help it can get in building its false immortal center.

One would never know from the way we use it that memory is there to remind us "fire bad!" or where you put your car keys. We use it for those things, sure, but we also use it to filter perception in our quest for permanence.

When you approach another through the fractured looking glass of your memories you can never truly see who is before you. You can never meet or relate with another as either of you truly are. Both of you come together behind scrims of memory and communicate through images of the past. Your past dictates how you perceive another and vise versa insuring that you never meet at all.

When you greet another with your memory up front you interpret the other's intentions according to your accumulated experience. You form immediate unspoken expectations that they have to overcome for you to feel at ease. If there is something wildly wrong about them (or you) alarm bells go off and you protect yourself by terminating contact. Generally speaking the other "acts" exactly as you want her to. You mold her. You decide what to remember about her whether it be compliment or insult. This is why some people gravitate toward abusive relationships while others don't. Neither is interested in healthy relationships, they are interested in vacuuming pieces of the other's past that strengthen their sense of themselves.

What happens when you stop acting from the past? What happens when you greet another not with the judgments from memory but as the stark, true beauty that they are? You will find that where it takes two to build a stale relationship it only takes one to Love. It only takes Love—true Love—to melt away those mutually strengthening egoic images and get to the real core of the human in front of you.

Oh God, I feel a quotable moment coming on... wait for it. Wait. For. It.

Flash light in the darkness you get light. Flash darkness in light you get light.

And you can take that to the water cooler.

Humans Are Conflict

Are you getting the sense that you are conflict yet? Not in conflict but conflict itself? I'm going to drive the point home through a specific example so it's easier to see. Then later, in Chapter 10, the same type of relationship scenario will be repeated but applied to a new angle. I'll apologize for the repetitive nature of this book then. No point in doing that here because you're probably not sick of it. Yet.

So here's a human touch to help you understand this and make the black ants running on the page look like words again....

I have a gal pal who recently came to me with boyfriend troubles. She is dating a man she says is "one of the good ones." As a result she finds him boring. She confided that her past relationships with men had been tumultuous at best, abusive at worst. This new boyfriend tried to show her that she mistakenly equates conflict with love as so many of us do. The problem is she already knows she does this and that knowledge doesn't stop her from finding bad guys more appealing than good guys.

In theory she likes good guys. That's who she says she wants for herself. But in practice it's the baddies she desires. Now she's asking me if she should repress this or break up with the good guy.

Sound familiar? Sound like anyone you know? Sound like anyone you are? Why are we such masochists?

We have tricked ourselves into believing that our personal psychological baggage is the root of our problems. It's a stem, I'll give you that, but the root? Not so much.

We have further tricked ourselves into believing that we live in conflict as if this conflict were separate from us, something we could escape in time. The fact is we are not *in* conflict; we *are* conflict. Our existence is conflict. In my friend's romantic relationships this elusive fact surfaces like the Loch Ness Monster anytime she scores a good guy. When she tries to have a relationship with one she realizes it's a mistake. She's not attracted to him. She knows she should be, it's not his fault, she feels guilty, she gets depressed, and then she wonders what's wrong with her that she's addicted to bad guys. Wash, rinse, repeat.

I submit to you that she isn't addicted to bad guys; she is addicted to achieving. Not achievement, *achieving*. The gambler doesn't gamble to win for winning ends the high. The high comes from the act of gambling. This is a modern version of the thrill of the hunt. We are all like gamblers and hunters where romance is concerned. And what we hunt is what we identify with.

When my friend says she has a goal, a hope, a dream of one day finding Mr. Right she's lying to herself. Her high lives in the process of finding him, which translates into dating a bunch of bad guys until she dies or moves on. It may hit her someday that she needs to settle down with a good guy. Abandon the hunt and settle even if that means boredom or eventual divorce. Given enough time she may come to see those as better payoffs than abuse.

So she'll settle and put her energy elsewhere. She'll find another outlet for conflict because she is that. Trading circumstances like this is no different than a drug addict swapping drugs for a different high. How does she get herself out of this life? How do you?

We need to decide what we want to do: understand ourselves as conflict thereby ending it or spend our lives upgrading our psychological baggage. When we understand ourselves as conflict there no movement toward or away from a solution and that is the solution.

See this. If you see this, you may not need to finish the book. You are conflict. *That is what you are.* To remain as you are you lie and say you are a (good) person who happens to be conflicted. Then you move to find a solution or give up and become a glutton for punishment. Both of these create conflict and they are meant to.

Yes, even seeking a solution is meant to create conflict. It is not meant to find a solution. You say you want a solution. You want peace. You want to be happy. That is a lie.

That is a lie, that is a lie, that is a lie. I cannot stress it enough.

Admitting this because it's true and not because you want a result creates the result. Understanding that you are the problem, not a person with a problem, dissolves the problem. Understanding kills it. Kills you. You don't want to be killed. And so... you lie.

And then something about apes. Did I get off track here or what?

Our Purpose

The history of humankind is the history of growth through ego. You might argue that the dawn of civilization with its evolving artistic and technological expressions was an amazing feat and we should be proud of ourselves. A growing tumor might make the same argument about itself all the way up to the moment it kills itself by killing its host.

Our self-expressions, entertaining though they may be, are a cry for reconciliation between the conscious and unconscious minds. This is not to say we need to regress back to the animal state, no. That's not freedom, although the animal has no delusions about growing toward freedom. We do. That sucks. Still, I'm not recommending regression.

What I am saying is that we have a purpose and it is not to live in awe of our accomplishments. It is not to cordon off the goodness we know we are deep, deep down in the suppressed depths of us as ideals to strive for yet never actually be.

Sentient beings asleep in their brain-conscious lives must awaken to the Truth of God-self to live as more than orderly barbarians. One must shirk off everything one's brain tells her. Again, this choice is what is meant by *free will*. It is often called the choiceless choice and we will soon find out why.

Comprehending the choiceless choice intellectually does not awaken you to Truth. It does bring you that much closer to choiceless surrender if you don't concentrate on the fact of the choice and make an intellectual game of it, which is the brain tricking you into believing you're on the right path. There is no right path for there is no path. There is the awake and the asleep. Simple. Words always are.

Now tell your brain to shut the fact up.

CHAPTER 5
What Truth Is

The psycho-spiritual aspect of us humans is like a funhouse mirror reflecting the brain's warped image of its environment. The image is neither complete nor real.

In the previous chapter we talked about the transcend and include principle but we left out something vital. In such a chain of being the higher domains contain the lower but not the reverse. To stick with our examples in physics, the molecule contains the atom but the atom does not contain the molecule. The cell contains the molecule and the atom but neither of the latter two contains the cell. Humans include this material principle in their nonmaterial spiritual hierarchy. In so doing we remain blind to ultimate Truth: All (and not-all) emanates within formless awareness.

God is the electron, the atom, the molecule, the cell. God is you no matter who you claim to be. God IS. Why settle for working your way up the hierarchy to find out that there's no hierarchy, there's just what is?

God Is Not A Tradition

I warned you before that a lot of this would sound familiar. Much of it has been mutilated by organized religion. If you're of the Jewish, Christian, or Muslim faiths this God we're describing may sound like the biblical "I Am." There are two dilemmas in comparing what we're learning here with what we've already learned in those traditions. First and foremost is that, as stated earlier, you're avoiding the issue by harkening back to them.

If you say, "Oh, that's the 'I Am' I read about in Sunday school," you might feel reassured by that. If you believe in a faith you feel comforted because these words reinforce what you believe. If you are not religious they reinforce that nothing new is being said. I'm spewing the same old dogma that turns you off so you can safely flush this book down the toilet and have not missed anything. In either case you remain as you are.

The second dilemma is that it actually isn't the same thing. Jews, Christians and Muslims—all the religions on their own terms, but let's pick on those three for now—are wrong. *They* still don't see that there is no *they* separate from *I Am*. If they did they wouldn't identify themselves by a religion and they wouldn't call God a parent.

Religions add direction even in their highest unorthodox mystical practices. The word *religion* itself implies a path. You can map out a way to live that best suits the needs of the culture or observe and compare how groups live—how the whole of humanity has set up the rules to its games—but you can't do that with Truth. Truth has no map. Truth is not the game of the nested hierarchy, the chain of being. Truth is not a study.

Truth, Facts, and Force

Truth. Do you hear that word and shudder? I do. It's meaningless in the way we commonly use it. It's one of those words like *god* and *love* that we just sort of say out loud and assume everyone knows what we mean. So let's revisit the definition we touched upon in the Introduction, that way we're literally and figuratively all on the same page.

Truth is implicit order and the force delivering it. This order informs the universe at large and the individual actions of one who is God-alive. Because God is all of being (including, therefore, all action) we can say that Truth and all the various words for God (Spirit, No-Thing, Formless Intelligence, Ultimate Intelligence, etcetera) are interchangeable. From the point of view of

Truth there is only Truth. However, from the point of view of self, or the time-stream, there is a breakdown of aspects. This, you'll recall, is a necessary illusion. We generally call these illusory aspects *facts*.

One difference between facts and Truth is that facts are malleable and Truth is absolute. Fact is like Truth's mirror: it reflects an image of depth and clarity, but at the end of the day it's just an image, not the real thing.

From our perspective, Truth is force. From the standpoint of physics that means Truth informs and gives movement to energy. It is also the force behind organic systems, the force behind instinct, and the kundalini force that feeds deep insights to the brain and healthful instruction to the body. We'll get into that later. For now, insert a *Star Wars* joke here and let's move on.

Since you are God and God is you, you are what gives fact its malleability. For instance, did you know that in physics, the particle appears to react in accordance with the expectation of the observer? True story. Nobody knows why. Well I do. It just hasn't been scientifically proven yet.

It is because the observer is internally divided into the conscious and the unconscious that the particle appears to respond to her thought as an object separate from her. The perception of separation comes from a flaw in the observer. In Truth, observed and observer are one.

The observer, if undivided, transcends and includes the observed in such a way that she may influence its very makeup. Animals and insects cannot do this for they are alive but they are not sentient. True though this may be, we haven't discovered it as a fact yet so it isn't real to us either.

Confused? Let us leave physics for later and try this angle....

Truth is the aliveness of *now*. Humans are like Medusa where Truth is concerned: by gazing at Truth we turn it to stone—we turn it into fact. Because we live in time the act of perceiving Truth draws it into time.

See?

We draw the timeless into time, make the immaterial material, thereby killing it, or to stick with the metaphor, turning it to stone.

From this rock we move, seek, and explore. We hop rock to rock unaware that the rocks were alive until we perceived them thereby submerging them in the time-stream. The rocks that we hop to—call them our future rocks—are nothing more than the murdered ever-present moment.

Time is the murderer of *now*.

Traveling on a spiritual journey is not progress for there is in Truth nowhere to go but deeper into our own fabrications. *Now* is all there is and all that is. We are therefore murderers of all that is. We kill ourselves; we kill God moment to moment, fact to fact, stone to stone, movement to movement.

Sentience

I introduced another word a while back, I don't know if you caught it. That word is *sentient*. *Sentient* means God-alive, which is exactly what you are when fully awake. All creatures—all matter and force—are God, yet only the vessels running on God-self awareness can acknowledge this.

Conscious humans like you and me live from the brain's point of view. Sentient people live from the point of view of God. Live from it, not just get a glimpse or a taste of it. When the sentient transcended brain-born consciousness, God became them. That challenge is what brains like ours are for.

We need to be clear on something else in this stew of words. Truth is not Truth because I say it is. It simply *is*. What we call *Truth* is not just another reality tunnel. It's not a different belief for which you trade in your current ones. Unlike reality tunnels, you are not trading in anything. It is not a matter of upgrading your standard of beliefs or even changing them entirely, for that is more accumulated experience fortifying you. In Truth there is no accumulation. If you were taught differently, then please do see the problem is that you were taught at all.

You were taught. You were taught things about the unknowable. You were taught to know the unknowable as a means to keep that initial woken ape fear repressed and therefore keep you, the ego, the persona, at the center of the universe. You got scared, went to your happy place and never came back. And now you teach your children how to do the same. Thrilling.

Truth Cannot Be Taught

Look, this isn't carpentry or language or mechanics. This isn't riding a bicycle. What is there to teach? Once this is pointed out, the "teacher's" job is finished. What more can we add that will provoke you to stop seeking not because a book says so but because there is no other way to allow God-self consciousness to thrive in matter?

Some of you were taught to seek enlightenment or Truth. Well here you are, end of the road, and what do you get? The mandate not to stop seeking but to stop the seeker itself.

Some of you were not taught to seek but feel the urge to do so anyway because you suspect something is amiss with this reality. You're hearing the weak heartbeat of Truth pulsing through the static of fear and so you turn to this and turn to that looking for answers like a dog chasing its tail. Turn right or left too many times and you end up right back in this position of knowing nothing. And that's the perfect position to be in!

Some of you seek not, contented to live by the ethical code of your society, the morality of your pastor, your parents, your clan, your self, your fill-in-the-blank. Your sense of morality is based on what makes sense to you, grabbing what appeals from a plethora of sources.

None of you are locked into these cages forever. You can hop from one circumstance to the next and then settle there. Or you can live in a restless state, never settling for anything but never succumbing to *nothing*.

Meanwhile, as you play out your dramas, Truth lies beneath and through and all around, there for the brain to recognize when it's done running and fibbing. Truth is one all-encompassing sphere beyond spheres and you will never access it through your separations. You cannot drag Truth to your wedge of the pie because the wedge is not universal.

Unlike picking another reality tunnel, which is unfortunately what many of you will make of these words, Truth requires emptiness. This means dumping the answers, superstitions, and self-control. And that is something the brain must do despite your protests.

The Self Is Thought And Thought Can't Get This

Persona is nothing more than the conscious actor, the dominant thought in the brain claiming control over all other thought. This is unfeasible—you *are* your thoughts! There is no decision-maker separate from the decisions, no feeler set apart from feeling. What's more, this is an illusion within an illusion for the conscious actor who pretends to be in charge is actually controlled by the impulses she has repressed. All of that, the totality of it, is her, not just the person she thinks she is. This is a quandary and the only way out is to see it.

If you see that all thoughts, conscious and unconscious, are one field wrongly divided, then the wall crumbles. The fundamental problem is that you don't see it even if you get the concept intellectually. You want to keep it as a concept so that you remain intact as the center of the universe deciding what you think about it.

Heck, some of you don't allow yourselves the full bloom of this insight because you are enamored with all that logic has to offer. You have settled. You've drawn a conclusion that all conclusions will eventually be drawn by logical means, but comprehending these words logically is not enough.

Words are the plaything of reason. You can mull them over, debate them, extract what you like and discard the rest. No words enlighten. No words are Holy.

Reading an instruction manual, memorizing operational procedure, does not make one an inventor, but your true nature *is* Inventor. You are the creator-creation. Grow up. Stagnation equals death. Species death.

If you're completely cynical you may ask, So what? Species come and species go all the time.

Well, it's true that the human form is as all things are: God expression. The God-alive don't see isolated drops of water. One sees the ocean. If the drops fail the ocean fails. If we die off, we are God failure.

Oh, you didn't know God fails? Yeah. God fails. Perfectly, every time.

CHAPTER 6
Absolutes & Subjectivity

I suspect one thing some readers are asking is this: What's with the absolutes? This sounds dictatorial. You're not my dad. Get off me!

We're talking in absolutes because we are talking about absolutes. Dictators (and crappy parents) speak in absolute terms about themselves and their politics. They have hijacked the language of Truth to serve themselves the same way religions have done. It's tough to hear the difference because so many of us have been raised to believe that there is no such thing as Truth. We're told there's this tapestry of overlapping subjective experiences that gets modified through the ages, but that's it. And there's a popular fallacy that goes hand-in-hand with this, which is the notion that all views are equal.

So what is our sense of the real? It's mush. When you break through to God-self awareness you see that you were correct about the equality of views but in the opposite direction: All views are equally false in the face of Truth. There's Truth and there's everything else. Everything else is living a lie, so on that scale all subjective views are equal.

Because we live in the badlands on the outskirts of Truth, we must make better than/worse than judgments in our daily lives. To ignore good/bad, better/worse assessments in the ghetto where they and we reside is to repress them. That repression is not the key to the gates of enlightenment.

In the badlands, freedom really is better than dictatorship. Peace really is better than war. Harmony is better than discord. Religion-wise, interpretation is better than literalism but atheism trumps both. And here the term *better than* means a higher ideal, higher intellectual choice, a more insightful approach to making sense of existence and living in a world devoid of God-self awareness.

Fundamentals Not Fundamentalism

We've so perverted spiritual language that we shudder to think there's such a thing as absolutes. Speaking from assuredness is not arrogance; self-assuredness is and the two are easily confused. Also easily confused?—definitive language and paternal sternness. Some of us hear absolutes and immediately go to the Heavenly Father nonsense that has been drilled into our heads by priests. Then we tune out.

Keep in mind that when we utter the cringe-worthy term *God-self awareness,* we mean the self-awareness of the formless intelligence we proved exists prior to and inclusive of all things. Allah, Yahweh, Krishna, Shiva, or Zeus it ain't. When we say *absolute Truth,* we're saying the insights that become how and what our brains think when illumined with God-self awareness, which necessarily includes the caveat, "This is not to be imposed upon another." That's not to say that the enlightened must choose not to impose; it's to say that imposition does not work. It's not something that can. This is insight numero uno.

These unfortunate word associations are why we're defining shared terms instead of taking their meanings for granted as we do in everyday conversation. They are not granted. Love is not. Life is not. God, meaning, Truth, nothingness—we're exorcising the perversions of these terms, dusting off the absolutes. Therefore, you mustn't reinterpret any of this book.

Reinterpreting this is the first step in forming a religion helmed by you, the interpreter. If this reads like a great hypocrisy, like fundamentalism or zealousness demanding you not interpret a thing, I understand. These are the fundamentals of No-Thing and so we have to endure the drawback of sharing the language commandeered by faithful believers. We're talking fundamentals; they're talking fundamentalism.

Postmodernists Still Aren't Buying This

I can hear some of ya now still screaming in protest that we're unfairly slaying the postmodern sacred cow named *relativity*. Postmodernists maintain that reality is comprised of subjectivities alone. They will confidently argue that objectivity is a myth. Reality is an amalgamation of overlapping points of view. They'll say there is no objective view even after having read this. Well what about that one? Is that an objective view? Is that an absolute? Is everything subjective except the belief that everything is subjective?

Postmodernist philosophers say there is no object about which we babble, just the babbling about the idea of one. Truth says subjectivity is born of time and objectivity has no relationship to this on its own terms. Objectivity is of the now. The God-actualized human is one who allows the objectivity of now to pour into the subjectivity of time like a waterfall.

Dark creatures can only guess at the nature of light. They settle for studying it and debating it instead of living it. When you live Truth, when it comes alive in and as you, you immediately see that you were using the wrong tools for discovering it all along. Until you see it from the inside you cannot know that the suppositions upon which your questions are based are wrong and so you're asking the wrong questions, making the wrong arguments.

To confuse matters further, when someone comes along and makes the unwavering statement "I do know," it's either a lie or a trick. If it's in a religious or dictatorial context, it's a lie. If it's someone who is enlightened, it's a trick. The trick is that the enlightened one does know Truth but part of that knowledge is the fact that telling you what she knows will not enlighten you. It will further create delusion, because now you're in a position to believe what the enlightened one says or not. You become a second-hand human being living in relationship with those revelations.

Even if you discard the revelations you had to ponder them to make that call. Usually you discard them so that you can carry on as you are. Some people carry on as they are and pay no attention to any of this. They settle. They are content to being the center of their universe just as they are, even if they'd never admit it.

Others carry on as spiritual seekers. They need to find Truth for themselves. They cannot have it handed to them by someone else. So the seekers seek even though the enlightened person who has "achieved" what they are looking for says, "Stop seeking. There is no way to achieve this. Seeking and psychological time must stop for enlightenment to be the case." Not stopping is how seekers remain the center of their universe. They, too, won't admit this.

The enlightened one knows all of these games and knows how her words will fall on deaf ears. She knows that taking her advice to stop seeking will not lead to enlightenment and neither will ignoring it for a life of complacency or a life of further seeking. On the other hand, she understands that a kernel of Truth must be preserved in thought for thinkers to have a chance to break through themselves despite the odds. And so she speaks.

When she speaks she knows she will be called a trickster if anyone is savvy enough to call her anything at all. Her language looks like a riddle, perhaps a nonsensical one, because Truth doesn't exist in answers. Answers are of the past. Answers are dead. Truth is alive as the now, as the timeless moment. Truth comes alive in us through the action of questioning properly.

Questions open us. Answers close us. We are taught to ask questions in anticipation of answers. It's as if we believe that perfecting answers equals more freedom. Nothing could be further from Truth.

One who speaks Truth sounds like she is speaking in riddles because that is how she remains open. That is Truth's language. Paradox is a form of it. If you embrace that language, if you try to wrap your mind around it, it disorients you, confuses you, dislodges you and that is perfect, for you are the thing that needs to be disarmed, dismantled, and dislodged. You are the thing in the way of enlightenment.

Our denseness often feels like it's being controlled by hidden conspirators in charge of keeping humanity asleep, but it's not. It's us. It's only ever us guarding our jail cell.

We're a dying race. Wake up.

Dying without resurrection—That's us. All of us.

It's sad to watch us go but the decision is our own. It does not get more straightforward than that, does it? Answers are always easy. It's the questions that baffle.

If I were a dictator I would save us.

CHAPTER 7
How Religions Happen

Speaking of being saved, there's one time-tested cage in the human zoo strong enough to hold all of this monkey business we call *seeking*. That cage is religion.

Religions the world over exist because the fearful brain needs to name the nameless and contain the eternal. The brain sticks to its cultural frame of reference like a skipping record, playing the same old song over and over again, because it seeks continuity and permanence through the self. Fearing its inevitable death, the brain projects a self that it then claims is immortal. Some cultures claim the self will experience heaven in an afterlife provided that it lives a certain way. The way is a communal agreement, which only strengthens the illusion that it's true.

The unknowable is an affront to us. We respond by manufacturing systems and structures in the form of religion. These religions try to capture the unknowable and grow stronger with time because we have no problem substituting the ancient for the timeless. When the ancient wisdom traditions feel old enough to be eternal, we trick ourselves into believing they are. In this way do we "capture" the eternal and keep that record skipping.

Let's get to the nitty-gritty of it: an enlightened one points out Truth. The people he speaks with are not transformed by his words. There is no complete metamorphosis within them, yet something about what they hear strikes a chord deep down, so they adopt Truth as a set of ideals. Ideals are a form of idolatry—of worshipping, or aspiring to be, that which you are not.

Ideals are also words to live by but not as. For instance, we have this ideal of peace. We are violent and we know we "should be" peaceful. Peace is the ideal; violence is the fact. Hope is the interval between the ideal and the fact.

Hope springs eternal because ideals are goals put off for a future that never comes. We must confront the fact of our violence not escape to the ideal of peace. We have to stop running from ourselves into the idealistic things we want to be because we are not those things. The hope that we will become our ideals keeps us shackled to violence. It distracts us from confronting what we are.

One who lives Truth speaks to us from the heart and those words become our ideals. They become the appealing thing we want to emulate. Ideals are Truth's dead carcass; they are more knowledge shoveled into the mouth of ego. Ego then vomits 'em out like poison. This poison is what we teach our children.

Through time there are rules made about these ideals. They become false truths for the people who believe in them. The one who initially pointed out real Truth gets deified. He's God or the Son of God. He's Buddha. He's whatever word any particular culture uses.

Testimonies, songs, and parables are written about him and his Godly knowledge. A committee of faithful chooses which stories to promote. Readers believe in these stories. Truth is lost to this mechanism.

The church is built. Splinter groups form. They have their own sense of meaning to pile on top of these stories, parables, and figureheads. Of course they do: It's only literature after all.

There are fundamentalists who read the words about the man-God and his wisdom. They refuse to interpret the words. They say the man-God spoke these words and since the man-God is essentially God in man clothing, we mustn't translate what he said or who he was. Of course the stories are wild morality plays that were written to be interpreted. The man-God was not a deity any different than any of us. The original words spoken by him came to this: "Be."

That's the central point any of the authentically enlightened religious figures meant to convey in their talks. To see clearly why this happens from the point of view of an enlightened figure, let's examine Buddha.

Buddha's Understanding

Buddha understood absolute Truth but he also toyed with relative truths. He understood that most people would not listen properly to the absolute— *properly* meaning in a way that silenced the listener's internal chatter so that Truth's energy had room to operate in the body. He built a system whereby the unenlightened may feel some inner peace while remaining fundamentally unchanged.

On the one hand Buddhism says there is no road to Truth. Truth just is. Stopping thought means waking to Truth. On the other hand it sets up a structure, a spiritual hierarchy from adept to master, and if you don't make it to enlightenment in this life, don't worry: Be a good person and we'll see ya in the next.

At first glance this may seem hypocritical or even a lie. However, contained in Buddha's understanding of the absolute was the anticipation that most people would not wake up. They would follow. For them he had a peaceful, rational system by which they could live.

If you tell a wounded woman that the power to heal herself resides in her ability to see through the pain, odds are she will think you're crazy. All she knows is pain. The wound is her life. So you give her some pain managing medicine instead. The medicine may get her to a point where she is in less pain so that she can think clearly enough to cure herself, not unlike psychoanalysis does for mental health.

The key word is *may*. *May* get. Why risk it? Why not cure yourself now and be done?

Getting back to Buddha, he knew that the Truth he spoke would get mangled and deformed and made into a system regardless of his telling the listener not to. That reaction is a natural outcome of revealing Truth to people who don't live it.

The lie was going to happen anyway, you see? So knowing that, he ingeniously shaped the lie into a system that is the lesser of evils. Not to do this, not to acknowledge the relative, would be to risk having Man turn Truth into cannibalism, for instance. Sounds horrifying but stranger things have happened. In fact that, itself, has happened!

So, yeah. Yuck.

If he had spoken of giving the self up and left it at that with a people who had no context for it, they may have responded by killing themselves or performing human ritual sacrifice. That he and others throughout the ages in all cultures have awoken to and spoken about this revolutionary perspective beyond perspectives in spite of the, shall we say, lackluster response, is no miracle. It's actually because the reality of it must be preserved in the mind of humanity like a time capsule waiting for excavators to dig it up when they're ready.

Absolute Truth On Its Own Terms

The reason we're barely acknowledging the relative here is because humankind has plenty of context already. We're drowning in relativity. We're finally at a place where we can hear this as it is because we've tried all the systems and they've failed us.

We are ready to hear the Truth, as they say. Not everyone but enough of us. Gone are the days of the so-called spiritual master having an enlightenment experience and bringing back from it knowledge for his or her people to build cultures on. Such a thing would be a mistake now. Arguably, it was a mistake then.

Look, every culture has their alleged man-God who utters one essential lesson: *Be.* But we'd rather discuss it than do it because to do it requires doing nothing and we are wired to do things. Can you image doing nothing? Can you imagine no movement? No thought at all? Can you imagine that?

By definition that is death. Do you want to die? No. You want continuity. Life is movement. Even though one points out that to fulfill our destiny as a species we must die an ego death, we refuse to take that leap of faith.

See, we've tricked ourselves, every one of us, all across the globe. It's just the natural reaction to one who speaks Truth. We take those words and turn them into wisdom. We hope that we can attain Godhead through the self or as the self. It would be another aspect of our persona that we are essentially in charge of. That's what we want. We want to be God as we are now with little fuss. We certainly don't want to take a backseat to God-self awareness.

"Want" is desire, "to be" is to put off indefinitely, and "God," by any of our definitions, does not exist. What in that is sacred?

Those who experienced it and came back to live like us showed us Truth verbally. Their examples didn't change us. Instead, we stole the language of absolutes and turned them into tools of repression. We put our faith in the traditions we made so we would have something permanent to fall back on in our insecurities over our impermanency. What could feel safer to people who have to die than a set of rules and conjecture about life and death written in solidarity to outlast death?

***

As we discovered earlier, Truth, being absolute, may sound like zealousness, dictatorship, or egocentrism. This is the fault of language and of description's limit. This is why one attuned to Truth enjoys silent bliss, which is the religious fellow's irritation. The religious need to talk, share, and convert. The strength of their convictions lies in approval from others and conformist vision.

But Truth just is and so there's no need to discuss it. One lives it, not discusses it. To take any further step beyond pointing this out is to invite disaster because further discussion breeds opinion, religion, structure, zealousness, competition, war—all the neurotic fruits of the lie.

CHAPTER 8
How We Kill Truth

Discussing Truth is Truth's death. Translating Truth is its death. Not living Truth is slavery, is to be dead inside and not know it. Such is the state of the world.

Religions are built on the original errors of doing instead of being, preaching instead of listening, and translating in terms of one's predilections. We were destined to make these errors. Fine. Now let's be destined to correct them. If not, then this book speaks and kills Truth in vain.

Truth Cannot Be Imposed

Let's turn our attention to something we covered briefly in Chapter 6. Truth is what one wakes up to and it is solitary. Part of what happens in that waking is the understanding that this cannot be imposed upon another. Truth has no relationship to imposition. One wakes or one does not. In the state of *does not* exist impositions. This is because we have no authentic inner instruction so we seek it from outside sources or listen to our own schizophrenic voice, which is the same, really.

The outside authoritative voice is the same as your own in that both are inauthentic. Just imagine what would happen if everyone who ever offered you unwanted advice on how to be a better person shut up. When they offer you advice they are talking to themselves. They are trying to convince themselves.

There is no bettering the self beyond a certain point. There is mental illness, obviously, but there are not dysfunctions within the ego that when fixed leave ego in a perfected state. Ego at its best is a trap. You are a trap. You trap and kill Truth moment to moment by your very existence. Again, don't feel guilty about that; it's no one's fault. It just is and it can end. It must end. Or humanity will. No pressure.

The Insurmountable Problem

Everything we do is a distraction from what we are. Our activities are designed to keep our focus off of *now*. Television, books, art, school, work, films, plays, sports, news—these are outer extensions of our inner turmoil. There are those in power who realize this and use it against us to keep us down. Lulling the masses to sleep is how they maintain power. Take something as innocuous as a shopping mall. Do you know how much psychological planning goes into a mall? Everything you hear, see, and smell is structured and regulated by psychologists to manage your consumer impulses. This one tiny, provable, tangible example doesn't speak to an evil ruling elite. It speaks to what citizens in a consumer culture think of each other. This is the power structure all citizens, be they haves or have-nots, play into.

You might be tempted to say the problem is impossible but I challenge that. The problem is only a problem if you allow it. Saying it's insurmountable is you running from it. You've never stepped outside of personal and social psychology so how would you know what's possible there?

The details of our oppression are like characters in a movie. There are thousands of them, right? Some are leads; some are extras. But they all come from one projector. Shut that off and they all disappear, including the people in power.

Power is agreement; it is a form of idolatry. I'll use me as an example here. I don't drink alcohol. I've had sips before at a wine tasting and at weddings, but I never experimented with it in high school or college and never drank as an adult. It just doesn't appeal to me. That is the whole reason why. There are a number of good reasons I can come up with but they are all after the fact. The fact is I don't like the taste.

American society is bombarded with advertisements telling us to drink. We're made to feel that there's something wrong with us if we don't. That's a lot of pressure, on teens especially, and yet I never succumbed. Why not?

It just wasn't my thing.

If it's not in you to do something, to behave a certain way, none of those influences work on you. They have no power. They hold sway over others but not you because power is an agreement and nothing more. This remains true down the line of issues be they broad or personal.

Self help books talk about personal empowerment but that's more of the same. Any action beyond understanding is conflict. This is the beautiful, simple fact. The fact is simple. The living it is a total revolution from how one normally lives. It is work, this elegance, and it rubs against the grain of everything one is taught. Going against the grain can also lead to conflict if you let it. You will do everything in your power to stay the way you are, which includes telling yourself you get this and are abandoning power. The antidote is to realize that as it's happening. Just watch it. Watch your reactions, your feelings. Physically, mentally, the whole thing. Watch without getting involved.

Can you do that? Can you watch your reactions without judging them? Without saying, "This is good; that is bad."

Can you stick with one question: "Is this part of the game to stay as I am?"

The answer may be *yes* every time but ask to find out. Don't assume the answer just because it was yes the last thousand times. When the assumption of an answer becomes the answer, it's not flowing from the innocence of the question. It's coming from you. When the answers come from you, you're right back at square one. This inevitably leads to frustration because you're not getting anywhere. You predicted where these questions would take you and they didn't. Clearly you did not ask them innocently but odds are you will stop asking the question rather than see the fact.

When you have an answer in mind that doesn't bear out is when you say, "Screw it" and meld right back in with the flow of society—the flow of power. That decision is full of angry resolve, which is a not-so-classy version of self-empowerment. Truth has no room to move there. This is stagnation, our stagnation, and stagnation is death.

Truth never dies and yet we've been saying that we kill Truth moment to moment. That's just how it looks from our perspective. You ready for a mind-bending twist?

Truth is movement and when we move on our own outside of Truth, we are stagnant. When we stop moving—which is the beginning of listening—Truth's movement is revealed. Consequently, our self-perpetuated movement is stagnation and so it is we who have died, not Truth. Died without resurrection. We are in limbo haunting a world of corpses. And this we call human nature. This we call a learning experience. This we call growth.

We name it to ignore it.

CHAPTER 9
The Recap That Moves Us Forward

Nothingness manifests all things as expressions of itself. One of those things is an organism that can and must further manifest the self-awareness of nothingness through itself. That organism is the human and so, much to the chagrin of postmodernists, human life does indeed have an objective purpose, which is to usher the self-awareness of formless intelligence into form by vacating the premises.

But not as an historical ascent! Let's be clear about that. There is no Spirit descending into matter and ascending to self-actualization via humanity through time or cultural evolution. We've set it up that way as a means to never wake up. Living in the delusion of spiritual progress is the only way we can remain in control of these here bodies and still feel like we're evolving.

Let's shout this one more time for the cheap seats....

We engage the world from the point of view of separation. The person you claim to be is a product of the brain. You are brain-based self-awareness as opposed to God-self awareness. Remaining a body-based self is the only free will choice there is and you choose it every moment.

Originally, the creation of body-based self-awareness was not a choice, it was a reflexive reaction to the new circumstances of no longer being a mere animal. The human brain *woke up*. It transcended the animal state. Transcendence doesn't mean that the former state disappears; it means that it gets enfolded into a larger emerging process. The animal is still in us and it's the easiest thing to identify with because it's immediately obvious. The gross physical world and the inner animal that you just were are the easiest means of identifying yourself and making sense of existence because they are accessible.

The animal *woke up* from *animalness* and felt terror beyond comprehension. This was instantaneous and appropriate because everything it just was had revolutionized into a new sense of being.

Fear divided the new mind in two: conscious and unconscious. Because the human latched onto the obvious and formerly superior aspects of herself and was overwhelmed by her new sense of environment, her purpose got repressed. As a result, the human to this day spends her entire existence chasing that purpose and rarely knows it. She cannot act. She can only react because authentic action is always new. It takes place in the now.

Hey, wait! Authentic action? That's a fresh term. I thought this was a recap?

Very good, Reader! I thought I'd segue us into new territory. Ya caught me.

Authentic Action

Authentic action is Truth's action. The human lives in time both physically and psychologically, so she can only ever draw on the past to inform her actions. Humans needn't live in psychological time. That is one of those early inevitable mistakes that take place when species wake up and identify with the obvious.

Humans experience physical time, or lifespan, and internalize it, emulate it, by creating a psychological past, present, and future. Psychological time is not real. It is the means by which the human brain represses its purpose, which is to reconcile formless self-awareness and form. This results in the human ego substituting itself for God and setting itself up as the center. The ego never understands the original fear because to do so means dissolving itself. It means waking up out of itself the way the animal woke up out of itself.

So the ego remains the center of the human. It creates outward expressions of the human's repressed purpose. For example, it feels guilty admitting that it's a false god, if you will, so it passes the buck by concocting religions and idols of worship to endow with its own power. It projects desire and hope onto them, which is further repression.

Tricky bugger that it is, the ego also creates inward expressions of the human's repressed purpose. For instance, if the ego does intuit that something isn't right with itself but finds no solace in those delusional external answers, it will search inwardly for an answer through meditation, psychoanalysis, hallucinogens, and so forth. It deludes itself into thinking it is different than, or perhaps better than, the type of person who creates outward expressions of repression, often believing that other person is too shallow to even acknowledge a problem. The shallow person will never "get it," will never broaden his mind. Or so goes the fantasy of being better than.

This is not to say there isn't a qualitative difference between the thinking of the literal-minded person and one who comprehends subtext. The fundamentalist, the literalist, has less mental freedom and so tries to mold the world within these horribly inept restrictions. He impedes ongoing evolution by constricting it to a finite object, usually a book of ancient rules. These are not equal minds. That's a legitimate division.

However, the outward mover is the same as the inward mover—the literalist is the same as his antithesis—on this ultimate level we're discussing. Both are reactionary and are stuck playing the game of translating instead of transcending, otherwise known as the game of states and stages. (Not to be confused with Chutes and Ladders.)

There are smart and inept ways to play but it's still a game. It's still a means to remain in control by slowly climbing to new heights and exploring each landing as your hardly fazed brain-based self.

The inward mover reacts consciously while the outward mover reacts unconsciously. Both live in psychological time. Neither truly wants to transcend themselves. The difference is that one may have this conversation with the inward mover fairly easily but the outward mover usually will not hear it. That said, here comes the swerve....

The Fallacy of Introspection

What I just wrote sounds optimistic, right? Like maybe the inward movers are not unfazed by their explorations and have a real shot at this ultimate transcendence thing.

Sorry, no. That's the fallacy of introspection and broadening your mind. Allow me to explain in story mode....

One fine day the outward mover decides that all of this religious hocus-pocus he believes in is nonsense. He perceives that there is something unfulfilled in himself and everything he was raised to believe just isn't getting at it so he chooses to explore some inward paths. These paths really open his mind. He feels born anew for a while but eventually that same old feeling creeps back in: there's something missing.

That original dilemma has not diminished; it has simply been covered over with new experiences and insights. The problem isn't the mover moving outwardly or inwardly. The problem is the mover. What does the mover do? What is the function of the mover? To move, right?

The mover moves through time. Movement and time are inseparable. They are measures of each other.

Physically, we have to move from point A to point B and that takes time. Mentally, we do that as the outward mover and/or as the inward mover.

Moving. Creating time.

Time begets itself. It's like envisioning a destination but always laying down more road so that you never get there. Why do you do that?—Because that is what you do. That is the function of you, the ego.

The ego is the thing that runs away from that initial fear inherent in the waking process. It is a virtual reality program that doesn't want to die so it creates and creates and creates in all directions—religion, psychoanalysis, *Friday The 13th* films—everything you do is a means of remaining in amnesia for you have identified yourself as that amnesia.

Slaves To Direction

Let's change the terminology a bit and see if we can't get some of ya to stop scratching your heads wondering what the heck you signed up for here. Trust me, I understand. This is not easy stuff and all of it must be approached from multiple angles. Think of it like going to the eye doctor for glasses or contact lenses. She puts that phoropter in front of your eyeballs and flips the lenses on it asking, "Better one? Better two? ... Better one? Better two?"

It's monotonous but necessary. This is cheaper than glasses. You'll thank me later.

So, okay. How about we call these inward and outward movers "directors" and see if this comes into sharper focus?

Director A is a fundamentalist. He is directing, which really means playing God, but he doesn't know it. The odds of that person reading these words and saying, "Holy crud, that's me!" are minimal at best. In fact, to Director A these look like the words of the devil.

Director B, who allows herself more inner freedom than Director A, is doing the same thing—directing. Unlike Director A, however, she acknowledges this and says, "I shouldn't be directing." After admitting that to herself, she steps off the outward religious path and onto the inward contemplative path based on the guilt or the intuition of the "I shouldn't."

Unfortunately for her she is still directing, still playing God, because the direction is not the problem, the existence of the director is. Although a better conversationalist at dinner parties than the fundamentalist, she is quite possibly more rigid in her delusions than he who never abandoned fundamentalism, because she believes that she has overcome the need to direct. She's the type of person who says arrogant things in likable ways such as, "I'm in tune with my higher self," or, "I'm in tune with the universe."

Sorry, Director B. You may have a greater sense of freedom in your life than the fundamentalist, and that may be healthier within guilt's game of "shoulds" and "should-nots," but ultimately there is no such thing as "should" and "should not."

The inward director's chains may be longer than the outward director's but both are slaves to direction.

We have to stop directing, stop moving, if we're to wake up to the now. Expanding our minds is just a form of procrastination because the director, the mover, the ego, is inseparable from the directing, the moving, and time.

"If time stops, the ego dies. I die. I don't want that! I want to exist," you scream.

Quite the conundrum. Yet once you see it, not just logically, but deep down in all your being, it's finished. The change takes place. You die.

Only then do you know what it means to be alive.

CHAPTER 10
Moving Beyond Psychology

Perhaps now it might be helpful to illustrate how it is that some ways of thinking are higher or transcendent of others but how what we're discussing renders that hierarchy moot. Let's stop picking on religions for a moment and push around psychologists.

It's better to understand your psychological dysfunctions than not. And people spend their whole lives in therapy discovering the reasons for their problems. That is healthier than pretending you have no problems and doing nothing to solve them, no question. But remaining in therapy you get the sense that discovering all the individual causes for individual problems isn't going to cure sorrow. Eventually, if you are perceptive, you will realize that the reason therapy isn't totally satisfying is because you are the underlying dilemma. You are not separate from your problems; you are the very root of them. You're conflict remember?

Let's flesh this out with a broad example. At some point in your life you feared you were ugly, right? That's universal enough. If not, pretend there's an ugly-feeling Bizarro You in an alternate universe who handled the insecurity thus....

You went to a therapist and discovered you had low self-esteem. It's not that you're ugly, it's that your own poor projection of yourself is unattractive to others. After years of therapy you unraveled this problem and learned that self-esteem is a hodgepodge of other issues, most of which date back to early childhood. When in doubt blame the folks.

But realizing why you felt ugly only made you feel better to an extent and so now you're trying to figure out why you're still in the dumps. A new epiphany comes to you, same as before. "Ah-ha!" you exclaim. And that's not lame enough so you chase it with, "Eureka! The problem is that I identify myself with the problem. Answers only get in the way of who I see myself as. I see myself as an ugly person and even though people tell me I'm attractive I will sabotage myself to remain as I see me."

This is another step in your analysis. Now you feel relief. Revelation brings relief. It's temporary, though, because one pressure gives way to another. Every level in the hierarchy of personal growth presents unique challenges that keep you in sorrow.

You see that you trade one set of problems for another. Admitting that you are married to the problems and that searching for answers is only going to strengthen the marriage, you're stuck. In that moment of stillness comes another *Ah-ha!*

"Ah-ha!" you exclaim again. "Identifying with problems isn't the root of all problems. The root is that the human brain is wired a certain way with a limited template of emotional responses to stimuli. Thanks to parenting and environment in my formative years, the points at which these responses peak and flat-line are molded into my brain. I, like everyone else, am a set of probabilities, a set of tendencies. Deep down we are all the same. We all have the same desires, mood swings, dysfunctions, highs and lows. How we express them is based on what we were taught overtly and subtly as children. Babies vacuum information and that information predicts their childhood, which informs their adulthood. What a Mr. Spock-like revelation! I see this clearly!"

And indeed it is a strong, if emotionally distant, revelation. And, as it is our cycle, we find joy in revelation, which eventually gives way to sorrow.

Why? Why is no answer the final answer that sets us free?

We are traveling the human road. Traveling. When we get stuck at a fork we stop for a breather. In that breath revelation comes and guides us in a new direction. We branch off accordingly. So the root—the real root—of human misery is traveling.

Revolution Not Revelation

We have been trained to seek. But when you stop seeking what happens? Revelation?

No. Stillness. That stillness is energy. That stillness is God. That stillness is You. You don't know that so you translate it into revelation. Even with those "lesser" psychological filters broken there is the filter of the traveler through which the energy is obscured. My telling you this may feel like an "Ah-ha!" revelation, but it cannot be the final revelation. The final revelation must come from the brain that projects you, and with that, revolution.

The brain must be still for stillness to be the case. It sounds self-evident, and it is, but we forget it all the time. Not only that, we're often told the wrong thing. We're taught to discipline ourselves into silence. That's wrong because there is no you that can exist in the stillness. Trying to be quiet requires the noise of trying. There is only stillness when you not just stop trying to be still but stop, period. When the brain relaxes something new happens.

What this book is repeating until we're blue in the face is that when the brain sees that the *me* doesn't exist, it gives up the *me*. The very seeing it creates a new action in the body. Of course we can't successfully communicate this fact with someone who is so mentally ill that they can't hear us. Mental illness is self-absorption to the nth degree. It is nigh impossible to hear others when your own voice is so overwhelming.

So we aren't going all Tom Cruise here and denying the need for psychologists. We're saying one needs to get to a place in oneself where one can hear this. One needs to be psychologically fit enough to be able to hear and comprehend that the root of the problem *is* you— not *created by* you, it *is* you.

Let's look at another example. Say you have a habit of getting into abusive relationships. Fed up, you see a psychologist. Together you sift through old memories and pinpoint when, exactly, you learned that behavior. Having figured this out, you feel relieved. You alter your behavior accordingly, yet the problem recurs. That's not always the case, though. Sometimes you get over it but then the next issue to get over pops up in its place.

Why? What does that tell you?

It tells you the memory that sent you the cue to form an unhealthy pattern was not the root of the problem after all. Psychology only takes you so far. It "fixes" you, makes you healthier, and it takes a healthy you to realize that you're not real.

I'm not real? I was real enough when I paid you for this book!—I know, I know. Such abuse. Let's try one more angle....

The person who is aware enough not to blame her partner for her dysfunctions goes to a psychologist. She needs to change something about herself, right? But there is nothing to change! Reshuffling the emotional responses to her significant other may sound like real change but the deck of responses is the same. Plus, the shuffler and the deck are one—they really are!

The reason many of us repeat dysfunctional patterns in relationships is that we strive to recreate the experiences we identify as parts of who we are. So, for example, if you're a woman who says, "Men always cheat on me," ask yourself where that word *always* comes from. Not all men cheat but the ones you bond with do. This is because the problem of being cheated on is what you identify with. To not be cheated on would run contrary to the person you believe yourself to be. Therefore, you are not even attracted to monogamous partners.

Look, if I have a problem then I get help from a psychologist or a priest or a friend, whoever it is that counsels me. That person listens to my story, asks a few questions, and in the end surmises that the problem stems from my upbringing, a childhood trauma, or whatever it is. Some past experience that predicts me, you see?

So I am told that I'm in arrested development. A piece of me is trapped in the past like a ghost. The psychologist calls this the inner child. It's as if most of me is adult-like but there are these fragments of my persona stuck in juvenile detention. These fragments comprise my personal unconscious mind. It is this mind that informs my conscious actions—most of which are dysfunctional patterns stuck on a loop.

Most of us are like skipping records: we can't move on until we get clean. At least that's what we commonly suppose we need to do, but do we move on? Can we ever?

We move from one problem to the next, always eliminating problems. When are they eliminated? When does that process end?

It never ends. It becomes its own cycle. See the sneaky fact of this: You are a jerk. People tell you you're a jerk. They're all wrong and you're right until one day you wake up and realize, "Oh my God, I'm such a jerk!" It hits you what everyone else already knows.

Now you're out of denial. You go to therapy to work out how and when it became acceptable to you to be a jerk. You figure it out, have a good cry, and open yourself to further scrutiny. What else are you in denial about? All of these other questions surface but you work them through. You change for the better, yet there's still this sorrow in you, this void. You cannot get at it but you keep digging. You feel good every time a new insight into what makes you *you* reveals itself.

You feel like you're moving on incrementally. Baby steps. But there's still a nagging sorrow that never moves and the fact that these issues continue to pop up. Here's why: You've traded the unconscious impulse that made you a jerk for the conscious impulse to be a better person. The old impulse is denial. The new impulse... is also denial!

The deeper issue psychology doesn't address is that your emotional responses *are* you, not separate from you. There is nothing to change. Changing even to be a better person is denial of the no-action required to transcend that person.

Change is not change, because no-change is change. (Say that ten times fast.)

It is a fact that we develop through childhood experience. This is when patterns and habits form. We frame the world in a new context as a separate entity. As babies we think the world is an extension of us. Most of us transcend that narcissism when we grow. We realize that the world doesn't revolve around us, cuz we're in the world, right? That's growth. And our brain chemistry goes through periodic changes as well, most noticeably as infants, at puberty, and with the deterioration old age hands us. We are not denying these facts.

The thing we're pointing out is this: The events that create behavioral patterns are not the patterns themselves, and those patterns **are** you. You can examine your childhood traumas until you pass out but the patterns your traumas created are still you. They may lose their potency; some negatives may recede into the background of your personality, but they are still there. YOU are still there. The graphic equalizer is not different from its settings. They are the same machine.

The relief one feels through examining the inner child is the relief of the experiences losing their emotional charge. The inner child dissolves with the charge because the charge created the child. So you breathe a sigh of relief, maybe have a better or "more real" relationship with your parents, but life still sucks because the patterns etched into the brain are still etched and these etchings are you. Again, you think there is a *you* separate from these etchings so you try forever in vain to alter them, even if it means popping pills for the rest of your life. Yet there they lie like dry riverbeds waiting for the sweet waters of your next mistake.

Impermanence Can't Create Permanence

We want the key to permanent change and yet there is nothing permanent about the brain. Why should we expect anything it projects be permanent? There is no quick fix, no scheme you can hatch that leads to a life without sorrow. There's understanding the whole of this which affects its own change. Change follows naturally from full understanding or not at all.

When understanding occurs you will no longer exist. The body exists, yet it is not operated by the mask, by the *you*. Furthermore, the transcendent mind does not forge dysfunctional relationships accidentally. One who is God-self aware lives gloriously alone yet is never lonely. The torch of consciousness projected by an impermanent brain cannot bring about this revolution. It must burn through you with the power of the sun.

Logically you may get what I'm saying but words are a barrier in themselves because language is incomplete. It is divisive. It is necessary as a means of pointing all this out but that's where its usefulness ends.

You Are Your Actions

There is subject-object relationship inherent in sentence structure. This does not exist in stillness so even identifying ourselves with the problem is a form of separation.

We're like nesting dolls the way we keep pulling off psychological mask after mask, searching for the so-called *real me* behind it all. We call it *soul* or *my true face*, but that's just more thought. Who is looking at the problem? There is no secret hidden you acting out in devious ways. You are that deviousness. You are that psychological mask. You are the traveler.

You are your actions.

There is no separate person acting. There is only action. The rest is appearance. You appear to be different from action because you've been trained to see yourself in this way. You've internalized how the external physical world appears and operate from that misstep. If you see all of this—really see it—the drama disappears. It is incumbent upon you not to translate the stillness that reveals itself into further drama.

Same Song, One More Round

There's one more type of person I need to address and that's the person who was raised to be psychologically astute, always self-examining, perhaps even hypercritical of her actions. She is as she fears: still screwed up.

Everyone on earth is born into mental illness. The best we can be is less neurotic than the next person. Why is it that so many people who were raised to be sensitive to what I just wrote and aware of their own unconscious motivations are still mental messes? Could it be because they were raised to believe in the absolute value of self-examination? Could it be that such a person's means of denying God-self awareness is to play the game of wanting to change for the better?

And if you, Reader, are such a person you might be yelling, "I do want to change for the better! It's no game!"

Really? Or is that just the correct answer that you've memorized and continue to regurgitate?

See this: No one wants to be the bad guy, but that good/bad dichotomy is false. The good guy *is* the bad guy.

You say you want to be the best, healthiest, happiest, sanest person you can be. You want to be those things, which means that you are not those things now. You put off being those things for some unspecified future date so what does that tell you about who you are right now?

Are you not at least second best? Unhealthy? Unhappy? Insane?

Some of us read that list of qualities and make a joke of it. We think, 'Oh, that last one definitely.'

We laugh it off and on we go remaining the same and always wondering why.

Why do you think this conversation is so repetitive? Not just in this book but down through the ages.

The plain fact is we are selfish. Selfishness is requiring that all experiences, including relationships, conform to our worldview because we are afraid to stray from that view. Our worldview may be wrong; if so, then is any worldview objectively right?

If there is no such thing as an objective worldview, then Truth lives nowhere in us. And we know that Truth doesn't because we blocked it out at the dawn of humanity. We substituted false worldviews. We created a lie. We created a series of them.

The best you can do is hope that you're living the lesser of evils. Without your worldview, which can only be sustained by likeminded people, you must confront the fact that you blocked Truth, which means confronting the ultimate fear: death.

You must confront the big lie. The big lie is you. Where you exist, Truth is but an ideal.

When it comes to spiritual seeking all of our questions are various forms of the same question. We don't want to face that so we keep asking from different angles. Even people who are raised to question themselves don't get it because they were raised to do just that: to question.

Some people are raised to punch their neighbor in the face; some to shower others with affection, to win them over. And some are raised to ask why they act the way they do. It's all the same. They are selfish and this other stuff is a backdrop to their selfishness. They don't really want to understand who they are, even the ones who were taught to question their own motives.

We react from our backgrounds. What we do isn't action; it's reaction. Our lives are a constant reaction to childhood cues and genetically codified impressions. It is easier to tell a bully this because it's more obvious. The sensitive person, on the other hand, was raised to know that her life is a constant reaction to childhood cues. That is who she is. However, that knowledge is not the same as understanding. It is only the self in a more cunning disguise than the bully.

Our sensitive friend spends her life in therapy growing bored, rehashing her childhood and what her parents' actions meant to her not to uncover anything but because she was raised to believe that that's what she should do. She was taught that to be a good person means not hitting others and going to therapy.

Fantastic! You don't hit and you're introspective. That is more feasible than beating someone up and denying responsibility for your actions. More feasible in the sense that people must get along and not club each other to death. But it is every bit as unfeasible as the bully in terms of discovering Truth because the self lives in reaction to cues absorbed in childhood including the cue that says, "Know thyself."

Stillness

True action—not the reaction of the self we've been talking about—springs from stillness in the same way that all things spring from nothing. If there is no you to direct the action, who directs? What have you become? A revolution takes place in the brain. Ego dissolves. God breathes.

You are light in this dark space.

And it isn't dark because you haven't flipped a switch. It's dark because you are the switch that believes it is the one who flips the switch. That "you" persona is a broken piece of switch. When the brain fixes the switch the light goes on by itself. The light is the body. The light is God. Heaven on Earth, if you will.

Earth is Heaven expressed. Your body is the temple suppressed. All is God whether you wake up or not. God suppressed is still God. So are the consequences of suppression.

What do you make of a species that is given the gift of limited self-determination, only to use it to destroy itself and everything in its wake?

You wouldn't awaken an ape to sentience if all it's going to do is clobber you. Moreover, an ape self-programmed to clobber cannot maintain its programming and awaken to its full loving, peaceful potential. Such a beast holds itself back until it wakes fully or commits suicide. Those are its only real options.

What is one to do with us? What is one to do?

Alas, all things for such a creature.

CHAPTER 11
Is Anything Manmade Holy?

And now we bring this conversation to a screeching halt to talk briefly about ancient relics and old ways. I'm sure it will eventually make sense that we plunked this clunker down on the slick road we've been speeding along for ten chapters. But for now... *Rrrrrrt!*

Parallel Mind

Ancient cultures fused spirit and science in ways that we don't. Who am I to claim that the geniuses who melded spiritual insights into their art and architecture got it wrong about seeking epoch after epoch? They said seeking was the right thing to do, didn't they? Even those who warned against seeking had a pharaoh to believe in, a guru who taught them, or a Christ to whom they relinquished themselves. What are the odds they were mistaken and I'm accurate?

First, ancient architecture with its hidden meanings and precision is the creation of a mind parallel to our mind. The ancients weren't better or worse at masonry than we are. They worked a different degree of exactitude based on the focus of their cultural vision. Simply put, they thought about things differently. Some aspects of their science cross over into our science, most notably in astronomy. But nowhere prior to the postmodern age was there an internet, computers, cars, Gap jeans, or Jar Jar Binks. The idea of mass production is ours.

So, yes, there is precision craftsmanship to the Peruvian pyramids, say, but there is also precision craftsmanship with our mass-produced goods. You can argue that their precision was more multidimensional than ours. There were meanings involved, the fusion of numbers and religious imagery. Codes not just craftsmanship.

Is that enlightening? It's all in what you worship isn't it?

Their passion was for astronomy, astrology, and Earth; our passion is for economy and global markets.

They worshipped the sun. They concentrated on sunspot cycles, celestial alignments, and the vastness of the galaxy expressed in the heavenly bodies. Their vision humbled them. Ancient Egypt was built on the backs of a mighty slave force dedicated to mimicking the heavens on earth.

We worship money. We concentrate on global stock markets, politics, and consumerism. There is nothing humble about our vision. We exploit and enslave other nations in service to our greed.

Both are social forces with precision and codes and beliefs disguised as facts. Perhaps in two thousand years archeologists digging in our dirt will discover our money worship and laud our passion for numbers. Maybe they will deem Wall Street a sacred place and the New York Stock Exchange a holy temple. And maybe the tourists who visit the ruins of Manhattan will feel something deeply spiritual there because of what they were told we believed.

Sacred Texts & Power Objects

Geez, with all this Debbie Downer information feeding your brain you might be wondering if there's anything at all holy in this world. Short answer? Nope. Well, okay, nature—but we're talking about thought constructs and manmade stuff. It may feel like there's ancient power in artifacts and words but time is not impressive.

There is no absolute meaning outside of Truth. Once Truth enters the time stream it dies. Meaning dies with it. Texts and other objects are not ever sacred just as reflections of Truth are not Truth itself.

Bibles aren't holy. At their best they are mere descriptions of Truth laced with dated cultural and political overlay, so why do the main religious texts garner millions of followers over centuries? Ditto that for sacred sites like medieval churches and ancient pyramids. They do seem to hold a power. Can the power of such places or texts lead us to Truth? Fair questions all.

Explanations for the power and allure of sacred places, texts, artifacts, and rituals are many and can best be answered by pseudoscience. Hey, what would a book like this be without a stab at explaining magic with science? Welcome to the knife fight....

Dr. Gary Schwartz poses an interesting hypothesis, which states that every object contains a closed loop pattern of its interactions, a history of its relationships. He uses this to explain how, for example, psychics can get a reading from personal objects such as a dead guy's watch. It begs the question: if objects hold patterns of interaction, then can we overlay or overwrite them on purpose? Can we charge objects with magical or emotional properties or even change their physicality through intention alone?

Sure, if you can psychically manipulate an object's quantum superposition. The principle of superposition is that an object exists in all possible states until it is observed. The act of observation draws it into a singular state of being. In other words, things exist nonlocally and gazing at them localizes them. But those other possible states of its existence still "exist" as potentials and so if one were to enter a nonlocal frame of mind, one could choose another possible state for the object. One could, in effect, manipulate the object's physicality and purpose from the subatomic level.

Again, I stress that one needn't be enlightened to pull off such magical feats and no idol made worshipful by you or your favorite mystic is ever going to lead to enlightenment. The ancients sought then as you seek now. All that's changed are the names.

Ancient and modern people suffer the same struggle no matter their precision or coded language. The perfectionism is adornment. The struggle is seeking. Inwardly, outwardly—it doesn't matter. No direction bears answers. Meditation and yoga—staples of ages old and new—are tools for the inner architect. Practitioners garner healthy results such as mental tranquility, physical fitness, and psychic awakening, but these upgrades are not enlightenment and they can't bring you closer to Truth.

Even after reading this book many of you will continue to assume that meditation and yoga are better Truth finders than the tools used by religious faithful who seek God outside of themselves through belief and supplication. Unfortunately, they are nothing more than variations on a theme.

Ancient/modern; inward movement/outward movement: there is no better/worse in terms of waking, just variations of seeking thanks to separation. Separation is what you see and you respond accordingly. You divide yourself from oneness and then seek it.

Stop.

Through the informed silence that understanding yields, one sees precisely what bibles, temples, power objects, and rituals are. These things may gratify us, scare us, flatter us, make us feel safe—you know the whole gamut of manipulations used to keep us faithful—but in the end we're performing magic tricks.

The path you choose, at most, at its best, in all your good faith, will lead you to a confrontation with that God or that ecstatic peak experience you've been craving, which, in turn, reinforces your faith. It's a bad joke we play on ourselves.

Again, we funnel God-self through the filters of our ego selves. We paint the pictures that satiate us be they positive or negative. We imagine that if we accumulate enough experiences, forge out into the world, say "variety is the spice of life," experiment with drugs, sex, religion, and fine-tune our moral compasses, we will discover the great answers to life's riddles, or at the very least an answer by which we may live happily ever after.

Experience is not the key to enlightenment. Variety is not the key, nor isolation, nor accumulation of any kind. There is no answer, including that and this and forever this. Understanding blossoms in questioning. Understanding is an extension of questioning not an answer derived from questions.

The body has a beginning and an end. Truth has neither. This blossoming is how the infinite shines through the finite. We are all a beatific blossoming and when we are whole we are holy. It is beyond sad that we refuse this.

Is Artwork Divine?

Demystifying sacred objects may not jive with how you feel when you gaze upon masterful artworks. We've all seen some breathtaking manmade things in our lifetimes, right? What is it about such objects that speak to us?

Artwork is often a reflection of intuited Truth that has trickled through the psychological filters of the artist and onto the canvass.

Religious structures strike a chord in many because of their blatant replication of that which we've been told is holy. They are blatant. Literal. They capture what we've already imagined about the unknowable and regurgitate it back at us. The moviemaker, the sculptor, the mason, the architect, and the painter all confirm the illusory reality we've consented to by invoking feeling.

You could say that the appeal of this type of art rests in its ability to connect with our brains in such a way that assures us we're okay and for a moment we feel the tiniest sense of release. We come unclenched a bit inside, a bit unknotted. But because the art piece is reinforcing the lie of us, that knot reties itself even tighter and we go about our lives fortified in evermore certainty that we are living in the light of Truth.

Abstract art is different. Abstract art's appeal lies in its connection to the conceptual processor known as the right hemisphere of the brain. Abstract thinking is a form broader than literal so it feels freeing to access and exercise the right hemisphere. Processing abstractly frees one temporarily from the answers and rules the logical left hemisphere demands. In this freedom comes, for example, the spontaneous insight of an inventor.

Through abstract thinking an inventor may realize the mechanics of getting from point A to point B. *Eureka!* exclaimed, her logical brain regains focus. She assembles the needed components and builds from there. If she gets stuck in the process, she shuts up her logical brain again and listens for the answer from the abstract.

From where does the abstract brain draw knowledge if not observations in the physical world? And from where do those religious symbols, deities, and all that stuff some of us find empowering come? They must come from somewhere, right? I have a feeling we will find out next chapter.

I knew there was a reason I placed this chapter here. Glee!

CHAPTER 12
The Difference Between Brain, Mind, and God

Let's take a step back, waaaay back, to No-Thing. We divided the word *Nothing* with the hyphen to illustrate that emptiness creates and is fullness and got a little cutesy with it by saying, "See? That fact is contained in the very word itself!" Then we worried that this was an overwhelming amount of information so we left some things out. *We* meaning *I.* I did this. Sorry. Or you're welcome. Whichever applies.

What I neglected to mention was that the hyphen serves another function. It symbolizes the transition from nothingness into thingness. If thingness is matter and matter is groupings of energy collected, bound, and made solid from one ocean, then the hyphen represents that ocean.

The hyphen equals free energy. We now see that our clever word No-Thing is an equation in disguise, where:

No = intelligence intrinsic to nothingness
Hyphen = free energy
Thing = matter
No + Hyphen + Thing = God

Ultimate Intelligence expresses itself as energy in which all things manifest; that is what's known in some spiritual circles as *the groundless ground.* This principle is also expressed through humans because we are the Earthly organism through which God-self may yawn, stretch, fart, and awaken. The enlightened recognize as a stunning fact that through human stillness (the quiet brain; the formless mind) God-self becomes you.

Introduction To Mind

Let's talk a little about the word *mind*. As we place free energy in the middle of emptiness and thingness, we also place mind in the middle of nothingness and brain.

Mind is a nebulous catchall term that is defined by its subcategories. We need not go into them all. Instead, let's note that mind contains, amongst other things, archetypes. Archetypes are symbols and personifications that are both universal and human oriented. In fact, levels of mind are shaped by the marriage of universal and subjective mind. The details of the mechanics can be found in Chapter 20, but here's the basic gist:

The horizontal monkey bars that were erroneously called *higher stages of consciousness* are co-created by us. Once the stage fits a holistic criterion (one that includes logic and laws, not just nonsensical imagination) and is agreed upon by a society, it becomes its own construct. The construct fills its landscape with symbols, personifications, boundaries of internal logic, and other fun stuff that makes sense within its expression. This is analogous to a company of people using a shared vision to create a video game that has a built-in capacity to evolve. If you didn't know that before now you might have mistaken such a dimension for a god, an afterlife realm, a Jungian concept, an Alex Grey painting, complete garbage, or whatever else it is not.

Stages of mind unfold through individual as well as collective perception. Some of the stuff of mind comes to us through dreams, meditation, yoga, rituals, prayer, binaural beats, and so forth. Much of it comes as an epiphany when the brain is quieter than normal. By ingesting hallucinogens you can cheat and take the direct route to various states of mind that may or may not exist as fleshed-out, agreed-upon stages.

Let's put this into practice so you can see it....

Sometimes the absolute Truth of God-self leaks through the subjective barrier that is uniquely you. So do universal symbols and universal truths that exist in the imagination. The imagination here means formless possibilities—all aspects of God that are not physical. This includes everything from the next great invention to the absurd; the possible and the impossible but not the actual.

Say that one fine day some of the *possible* stuff that cannot be made material (because although it's not absurd, it can't exist in the exterior, physical world) comes to you in a dream or when you let your guard down, meditate, sit on the toilet—however it comes to you. And say it has the emotional jolt of thunderous Truth, so that you simply know it's the case even though it's not physically real. If you confide in others and it also rings true for them it develops its own life. If it doesn't it withers in your head or becomes art.

If many recognize it as self-evident they explore it. It unfolds as they explore. They are co-creating it; they are the gods of it unless they don't realize that and then it mistakenly becomes their god. It would be as if you were a dreamer and the dream but you so over-identified with the dream that instead of waking up, you manifested a dreamer within the dream who dreams other dreams with their own dreamers! (Say *that* ten times fast.)

All of this is bad news for atheists, humanists, and others who believe that a brain grappling with its own awareness of the exterior world, in ignorance of science, produces all the junk of religion. They see beliefs as placeholders for the things we don't understand because either we are unaware of what science has revealed or because science hasn't revealed it yet.

They aren't wrong about that, but they're only half right. We're not only grappling with the outside world, but the inside world, the interior domains we've co-created with universals.

Beliefs aren't solely about covering over our ignorance of material processes with the lies that feel good or give us meaning, although that is part of it. Beliefs are also developed around these interior domains we don't understand and it is here that science isn't helping. Materialists would reduce these domains to biochemistry if they could. Thankfully, emerging physics is snapping them out of that.

Interior domains exist for the same reason exterior domains do: because the whole of formless intelligence must exist as a reflection of itself and that means breaking the whole into parts within parts within parts. Once an interior domain has taken on a life of its own we approach it through shared perspective.

How mind works and its various uses could fill an entire book or three or four. Suffice to say that mind stuff exists for the same reason that physical stuff does: Because all things must be expressed.

There are lots of ways to access the toy box of mind. However, let's be sure to differentiate what we find there from enlightenment. For example, if your brain starts humming like an engine and your perception is suddenly immersed in an endless expanse of symbols or stars and planets within a blue entity, you may have achieved Krishna consciousness. But that still ain't it. You may think that's it, that you've arrived at God or enlightenment, but it's not. It's friggen cool to be sure and vivid and blissful, but immersing yourself in the virtual reality of an archetypal persona is yet another diversion.

Sorry, Hindus. It was your turn to get picked on. Hare, hare, hare.

That which comes from somewhere or something does not come from direct God-self awareness. Of course all things arise in and as God but true enlightenment is only concerned with connecting to the stage beyond stages, the actual point of view of God, not the point of view of the creations within God.

There is no movement to or from God, no spiritual growth or devolution. God is all, including states and stages of mind and including the denial of God. One must be still as God to hear this.

Archetypes

Let us put a magnifying glass to archetypes and see if we can't discover something so outrageous about them that it will sell more copies of this book. An archetype is an idea or pattern of thought inherent to humanity and expressed in each individual. The expression is primordial and therefore transcultural.

We inherit symbolism through ages of shared repetitive experience. That part is easy to figure out. The hard part is in understanding what the brain is responding to. What I'm about to tell you might be the most controversial thing in this book. Then again, probably not.

Archetypes are alive. Ours are born from the union between Truth and the symbol-processing brain living in denial of Truth. You, the brain-born self, cannot make direct contact with Truth. There must always be a barrier and that barrier is an image.

Truth is always there to be engaged by the brain directly, but as we know the brain blocked it out with self immediately after arising from animal slumber. Still, we new selves hadn't built up mind yet. We just had our selves and Truth's echo.

We never fully blocked Truth, did we? We killed the 1st-person experience as it but we had no problem cannibalizing its mandates when they came to us through 2nd and 3rd-person interactions. For the pre-logical ego to interact with Truth as a separate entity, Truth had to appear in the mind's eye as geometric shapes with inherent meaning. The brain formed concepts about them and those concepts become our collective mind—a further barrier between brain and direct perception of Truth.

That is to say, when Truth touches a brain that is blocking it out, the interaction forms mind. Archetypal geometric shapes are the fabric of it and archetypal humanoid characters inhabit it. The marriage between you and Truth as a separate thing you intuit is the circumstance in which thought-form offspring are conceived.

Archetypal humanoid characters are the next phase in the evolution of mind. When archetypal symbols are engaged over and over and their meanings refined, they become their own living, albeit nonphysical, entities with their own internal logic. They tell their own stories to us over and over again. We helped conceive these stories so the ring of relative and objective Truth keeps us coming back for more.

Truth is not a structure. It contains and surpasses all structure. However, when Truth is treated like an outsider it must take form. Since the brain will not allow Truth to become its own self-awareness, Truth must fashion structures with the aid of the brain through which it may speak to us. Therefore, archetypes are the middleman between Truth and the human.

CHAPTER 13
Religion 2: Electric Bugaloo

Now that we've discovered what mind is, it's time to take a look at some aspects of religion we've thus far neglected. What follows is a casual analysis of arbitrary religious miscellany that has stuck with us since days of yore. Whatever else religion has it has staying power. Political oppression isn't the only reason. Many things the religious do for spiritual effect work.

Zen Koans

Take Zen Koans, for example. What is it they actually do? They alter brain function by having the practitioner ask paradoxical questions over and over until the logical left hemisphere tuckers out. When that happens, the right hemisphere goes nonlocal in the brain's quest for an answer. If successful, it plucks an epiphany from the ether.

Epiphanies are realizations not derived from actively thinking but from the silence between thoughts. This is the basis for a phrase you may have heard a lot of in recent years, "the power of intention." That is where you concentrate on something hard (in the localized brain) and then let it go (into the nonlocal ether, or mindscape, or information field—these are synonymous.) This clench-and-release method is like casting a fishing line into mind: what you hook is an epiphany. Or, in the bastardized American consumerist version, you reel in a windfall of cash, cars, and romance. Oh wait, you don't? Shock.

Koans involve practice, which is repetition plus concentration. The self-disciplined mind is rubbish, being that it is divided. Divided mind cannot channel

Source directly. The friction and collision from trying are never the sound of one hand clapping.

Here's your koan for the day: To concentrate on the sound of one hand clapping involves two hands.

Belief & Faith

Perhaps you've wondered if there is a difference between belief and faith. There is. Belief is passive; faith is active. Belief is in that which has passed; faith is in that which we wish would happen or hope exists now.

Religious belief puts the brain in a type of order that allows it to rest. Even in its purest form belief is perverted because, although it may free up enough headspace to allow Truth to maneuver, it sets up parameters, an obstacle course of thought constructs through which direct perception is distorted. As with all thought constructs, belief serves ego.

People of faith have faith that their beliefs are correct now or will come to pass in the future. Faith gives life to beliefs, which are of the past, but one needn't hold beliefs to have faith. For example, many people switch belief systems on the faith that they will eventually find happiness through a system that's right for them. They have faith in what they will find not in what they have found.

If you're a Born-Again Christian you may be wondering how any of this applies to you. After all, you did experience the gut-socking blissful love that spread throughout your body when you gave over to Jesus. Love and forgiveness—the things of absolution— overwhelmed you in ways nonbelievers are left guessing at. That happened, didn't it? That was real!

It was real, sure, but ask yourself: What was real about it? Was it the association your church told you to make between this palpable cleansing love energy and their god? Was it the absolution itself? What caused that moment of blissful forgiveness?

You did. You absolved yourself of your transgressions by acknowledging in that moment that you are a fraud. As fantastic and real as that moment was, it's the next moment that really, really counts.

In the next moment, after the ecstatic feelings dissipate, you are now the property of another thought construct, which is the culture-creature Jesus of whichever denomination you've handed your life to. Feels great, feels authentic, but you're still you in subservience. You may even get militant about it, call it a sacred experience, and protect that memory at all costs from the infidels who haven't had it and therefore do not understand. Or maybe you leave the bravado to extremists and fight the good fight inside yourself, where you recall that cherished moment always.

Is protecting a memory a good thing? Is keeping it on life support through tradition, oppression, or personal certainty a good thing? If not, how are you working in service to the goodness you felt on the day of your alleged rebirth?

To experience the true miracle of rebirth you must embrace the cold hard fact of death, not live in the shadows cast by another's light, and certainly not regurgitate your own moment of blissful surrender over and over like a nostalgia junkie hooked on remembering when.

Don't swim in your vomit and tell me it's a clear pond.

Handing oneself over to a god of the people is passing the buck. If one could raise a child with no concept of God, that child would be God and there'd be no need for rebirth. This doesn't mean raise the child as an atheist or an agnostic. It means raise the child with no concept in any direction, period. Never a mention in the child's life. Such a child would not grow in the shackles of concepts, a slave to the self.

This Is Your Brain On Religion

Let's go deeper. Let's turn our attention to how different religions stimulate different parts of the brain in a way never before discussed. (Never before discussed?—Oooh! More added value! More book sales!)

In the throes of religious ecstasy the Christian feels forgiveness, compassion and love from God; the Buddhist feels the sweet release from desire in emptiness as God; the Hindu feels freedom from psychological bondage by learning a pantheon of Gods; the Muslim radiates honor, responsibility, discipline, and humility in prostration to God; and the Jew feels like God's chosen keeper of the covenant and of holy knowledge. When we give the self to a higher power, universal energy has room to maneuver in the body. Normally it is blocked off, suppressed by the me, but having given over the me to a higher power brings this immediate flood of energy through the body. However, the religious have not totally given up the me; they've given *over* the me to a higher power that isn't really higher at all.

What you call a higher power is another projection of yourself. What you do in giving over to the thing you've dubbed "higher" is eliminate all but a fragment of yourself. You don't recognize it as a fragment born of you because you just gave what you thought was all of you to it. The effect of this giving is a new and real spiritual experience, a rush of energy, so that seals the deal in your mind: God has touched you.

And why shouldn't you believe that? It works like a charm and is something the materialist, the humanist, the atheist, and the agnostic will never understand. The energy is real enough and truly cleansing. It is there, no longer completely suppressed; the nature of the suppression has changed. You acknowledge its existence but continue to dominate it by calling it Holy or God, or calling yourself chosen or blessed.

Here comes the part no one has said and it's the reason that the religious are so certain their religion is the one true path while all others are wrong.... On one level we make up stories about life and death out of fear. Through consensus approval these stories become the embedded systems by which we live. Now we're adding this epiphany: When we break through enough of those illusions universal energy flows through the body. However, because the religious give the self over as opposed to giving the self up, they take what is universal and tailor it to their specific expectations. This doesn't just happen in terms of forming a vision of what God looks like but also how God feels or how they feel in relation to God. How this plays out depends on the emotional imbalance inherent to the religious teachings they have absorbed.

When the Muslim feels that "higher" calling it is because universal energy is channeled into the overblown sense of duty he was taught to emote. When the Jewish mystic flows with universal energy, the predominant feeling is of being the Chosen and his intellect floods with insight, with "secret" knowledge.

The expectations of our religious teachings carve out a lakebed in one quadrant of the brain. When we dedicate ourselves to those expectations that lakebed fills with universal energy. It pools there. Universal energy pools and its directives filter through the religious expectations. Absolute Truth dies and becomes relative truths. Thus the religious person's certainty about knowing the true path to God is due to a chemical imbalance in the brain.

Again, the so-called "higher power" is an aspect of the self that the self believes it is dying to. But it isn't dying to anything. The self is very much alive but it has put on a different mask. The self acknowledges the powerful new energy in the body but dominates it by saying it is specific, not universal. Control, control, control.

Another suppression of the universal is born. Another lie is sustained. Dysfunction continues unabated. This holds true even for those who espouse "the way of no way." It may hold true for you too depending on how you read this book. If you read it and follow it like a map you remain lost.

No Path

The Christian Mystic has the same experience of the Ultimate as the Buddhist monk. This experience is nearly indescribable. By jailing the experience within religious contexts, by laying down a path to enlightenment, we do a disservice to the spiritual seeker. Christians do not own enlightenment anymore than Buddhists do. These are merely languages various cultures use to articulate facets of Truth. They are no more paths than English or Spanish.

The word *path* is misleading. As stated, these paths are languages—faulty languages—and nothing more. These languages describe authentic experiences, which have come to pass and were never yours to begin with. Someone else's experience is not yours so stop seeking it.

Seeking implies finding. That which one finds is not God because God cannot be found. God isn't lost. There is no path, no way to find, nothing to seek. Since there is nothing to seek, the seeker must not exist except as a form of denial or retardation. When denial dies so dies the seeker. In that moment of illusion stripped the vessel that was the seeker seeking is now the being *being*. Being is the person; being is the action; there is no division in being.

Likewise, there is no divide between God and being. They are not a *they* for *they* are one. Explaining this in parable and metaphor we create religions through which followers mistakenly think they've found the righteous path to God.

Religious Tradition Is Spiritual Repression

A comparative analysis of all major religions may lead one to conclude that because they each describe some version of an ultimate truth, they all lead to the singular Ultimate Truth. We now see that this is wrong. Religious traditions are a cage built from the bones of Truth. The disciplines and rituals found therein are a means to force you to behave in a godly manner. But you cannot behave in a godly manner because you are not godly. This is another form of repression.

All manner of genuine, wholesome directive lives in the ever-present now and arises spontaneously in the body when the brain lets go the ego. Sounds fictitious but it isn't, and one needs no guru, no saint, no Christ, no Buddha, no other to initiate this. It's not that such a person cannot initiate this in you it's that the lie of their having tapped an ancient source or even the ever-present moment using ancient techniques comes with it. You adopt their lies because they performed the magic trick of awakening this energy in you. You follow their rules and receive wisdom according to their guidelines.

What is more true than anything the traditions offer is that certain of these things arise spontaneously in you in amount or degree appropriate for your specific needs. If you buy into the ancientness of it, the prescription of the so-called enlightened other, then you remain in the purgatory of attachment and self-fulfilling prophesy. Bliss states are not Truth. They are higher, broader, deeper forms of masturbation.

If humanity is one, then we are slaves to our separate selves and the fears they create. We are a murderous, ignorant beast with many arms and so one must ask the revered solitary monks of the world: What good are you doing working your practice in solitude? Indeed, you are also the problem having suppressed the harsh impulses reflected in the eyes of your ignored neighbors. All of us must claim responsibility for this human mess, as it is no one else's. There is no hiding from that. Not in a cave. Not in a monastery. Not in a god. Not in yourself.

Forgiveness

Since we're covering a number of religious bases here, and since we mentioned forgiveness, let's scrutinize whether there is any merit to it beyond allowing the forgiver a personal sense of well being or subtle conceit. Those are the average ways we use that word *forgiveness*, yes? And also, for Christians, there's that bonus definition in terms of asking Christ to wipe their slates clean and forgive them, right? Do these have anything to do with real forgiveness? Is there true forgiveness or just contrivances?

Eastern schools of thought maintain that we should be thankful for those who have wronged us and embrace the wrongs as learning experiences. No need for forgiveness there. It's implied.

Western conventional wisdom doesn't buy that but it does say we have a limited time alive and so we must forgive those who have wronged us lest they perish and we never get closure. Or we die without having unloaded the emotional baggage we've lugged around vainly. Who does carrying baggage hurt, the offender or you? Some may get this and live rightly by it but most, I'm afraid, don't. It's easier to hold onto hatred when time is limited.

"We all die anyway so what's the difference," some ask. Others go the opposite direction pretending to forgive out of fear that time is limited. Their forgiveness is actually a suppression of their ill will.

In Truth, as we know, there is no time. We have eternity and we have infinity. So the question is, do we want to carry these hatreds around in us forever? Eternity plus hatred equals hell. Hell is in you right now. Understand this with all your being, without judgment, without that barrier of fear, and see what takes over. That is all Love is. Love is ALL.

Forgiveness as an act is never necessary when there is not a division called *time*. True forgiveness is not an occasion it is a state of being. Those who live forgiveness need not proclaim their forgiveness to another. That's just putting on airs. Someone has poked at your ego and you forgive her as a passive-aggressive means to poke back. Forgiveness in this context means control. You control the situation, the other person, and as a bonus, get to feel like the better person.

Well real forgiveness is not an event in time. It is a byproduct of understanding. Those who live in understanding necessarily live in forgiveness. One emanates from the other as perfume emanates from the rose.

Hear that Catholics? Good news! You can stop going to confession now. The jig is up!

You confess your sins to priest or God for absolution because you are not in the fold. God, priest, or anyone forgiving you is you forgiving yourself once-removed. Your whole life is wasted sinning between breaks and the breaks are spent apologizing to yourself. The covenant is only ever made and broken within oneself.

Is Anything Sexual Unnatural?

Speaking of priests and sinning.... We often hear religious people talk about unnatural acts, don't we? Does that have any real meaning?

In America—in other places too, but it's practically a national pastime here—homosexuality is scorned as unnatural by the Church. Is it ironic or just stupefying that gays and lesbians have to fight for the right to get married because so many people consider homosexuality an unnatural choice—but not monogamy, which goes against our natural programming to spread seed far and wide? Oddly enough only one of those is a proven choice and it ain't lovin' yer own.

Sounds like I'm about to lay out a liberal political argument here, doesn't it? Oh, sadly, I am not, for in Truth, neither homosexuality nor monogamy are unnatural. They are, to coin a term, *unbiological.*

Nature evolves us physically and mentally. Humans experience life as an unfolding nested hierarchy wherein mental growth picks up where brain development leaves off. Clearly the brain/body is the projector from which the mental is projected, but the mental is no longer owned by physical drives, and so while the average twenty-something male has sexual fantasies every 10 minutes, that doesn't mean he has to seed as many women as the drive begs. It is biological to do so but at this stage, unnatural.

The argument against gays and lesbians, such as it is, is that it's a lifestyle choice. The blunt sex act can be. Most male prisoners who have sex with each other don't consider themselves gay. They're giving in to their sex drives.

But the very question of choice is a false one. It's unimportant whether homosexual sex is an expression of love, desire, brutality, necessity, or rebellion. The fact is it's not unnatural to do unbiological things. There is no universal right and wrong in sexuality between consenting adults. There is a range of freedoms we indulge in based on personal comfort. What in that demands persecution or legislation?

Choice is a tool of freedom, not freedom itself. When one steps outside all of this nonsense we claim is human nature one sees with perfect clarity the machinations of sex. From that vantage point there is no craving in any direction. Total freedom lives there.

Why do people who believe that they are more than their bodies get bent out of shape about homosexuality when it proves their belief? It proves that we can work against the reproductive programming common to all. Often this leads to healthier relationships for gays and lesbians. If I were looking for evidence that we're more than our bodies I'd start there, not eradicate it.

If, on the other hand, I were looking for Truth, I'd stop looking, period. If you read stories from an enlightened person as a "how to" manual, you will mistake the events that unfolded after their light bulb clicked on for a path to the light switch. This happens all the time. In fact, it's happening right now with priests and monks who repress sex.

Some religions talk about conserving vital energy and some talk about doctrine added by their papacy as reasons for asceticism. For some it's a means to appear above it all and for others it's a sacrifice to the higher. It's better to sacrifice dirty animal urges than dirty animals. Am I right, people? Am I right?

But here's the fact that boils under the surface of their explanations: Celibacy is deemed an indication of purity because the enlightened use sexual energy differently than the rest of us. They are not attached to sexual cravings and urges because they are not lacking anything. Seeing this, priests mimic the actions of the enlightened so they can feel God-alive in the way that one feels like a super hero after watching a super hero movie or reading a favorite comic book. It's an imaginary replication, the projection of what they've heard and read and seen and liked. As with any other type of wannabe they emulate the thing that appeals to them that they've not experienced. Because they've not experienced it, they don't know what they are doing but going through the motions feels cool.

When one's body is fully alive (a product of God-self awareness shining through it), the orgasm reveals its other properties, which include physical healing. The orgasm acts as a generator for the subtle system of energy centers overlaying the physical body. You've probably heard this system called *chakras*. An exhaustive examination of what chakras do is beyond the scope of this book. It's enough to know that they exist whether or not biologists have discovered them. You can activate them without blossoming into God-self awareness, but the full power and relevancy will remain out of grasp.

When activated by Truth, the new purposes of orgasm manifest in the body and the stranglehold these other desires have on us recede. There's no more attachment to them. The physical nature of the orgasm itself changes. No longer is it something that happens outwardly as ejaculate. Now it's internalized and the healing power of the resulting endorphins gets routed to problem areas in the body.

And so the real reason ascetics and religious types control their sex drives is to appear godly to themselves and the world because they don't understand that the drive takes care of itself in one who already is Godly. Perhaps they read in a book somewhere that to achieve God-self one must control physical drives. Or perhaps, like how the invention of the internet is a result of intuiting oneness as the case, they intuit the underlying utility of the orgasm and try to replicate it artificially. I don't know. I can't speak for them.

I only know that the real reason they repress is to remain themselves in the face of God-self. That is, after all, what we do. We practice self-control, self-denial, and call that a spiritual path.

We misunderstand discipline.

Miracles & Cynicism

But enough about sex, what about virgins? Specifically, the Virgin Mary. More specifically, visions of her.

Do miracles happen? What are they? It depends on what we mean by "miracle." There are several valid definitions. The word covers a lot of ground. One type of miracle in particular is worth a look: religious visions. These include Marian events, such as those at Medjugorje and Fatima, where the Virgin Mary comes to poor kids with a message for humanity. Is that sort of thing a culmination of hoaxes and mental deficiency or is there a Virgin Mary apparition who talks to paupers?

Simple answer: These are examples of God-self using cultural tools to address us in the 2nd-person/relationship perspective we're stalled at. It's like God's talking to God's split personalities (us) through further delusional intermediaries (our religious icons).

Look, aliens are God, angels are God, trees are God, breast implants are God—even you are God, but you turn a blind eye to it. Visionary phenomena are God-self speaking to brain-self as an outside agency in the context and language the brain understands. The messenger is the force of the breeze that carries oxygen, not the oxygen itself. We make idols of all these messengers because idols are tangible. We project them outwardly and name them. We have the opportunity to hear their messages in terms we can understand, but what we usually end up doing is translating their messages into what we want to hear.

We hear what we want to hear.

Then why do they come, these culture-form messengers? If it doesn't work, why bother? Fair questions.

Again: fundamentally there is no *they*. Just like a dream, there's only one dreamer conjuring characters and setting degrees of meaning and so forth. *They* come because that is what *they* do, often sounding like a broken record. The more entities who shout "Wake up!" the more likely one shall. After all, some people do see Truth peeking through the cultural façade even as the many around them bow to the façade itself.

Here we are at the end of the Age of Reason. Beings—angels, aliens, all higher non-human forms— are fantasy to scholars of religion and myth. These educated blokes assure the masses that belief is personal; objectively there are no other beings. Everything is explained away as a function of the brain and loneliness, neediness, wanting to feel special in a world of conformity, yet even this super rational age can't shirk off the messengers. And what is their message? Anything new?

No! It's the same tired crap! Thankfully now we're smart enough, logical enough, to say, "Wow, all this religious stuff is futile. I think it's time to wake up."

Still, in our see-it-to-believe-it nuts and bolts mindset we ask: Are these messengers real? And if I answer that some are archetypes and some are life forms who have passed through similar waking processes and are here as midwives to birth us into our full being, does that discredit this whole book in the eyes of the "prove it to me" skeptics?

Can I get away with saying, "The life forms behind the messages are as real as your form, but what's important is acting on the message, not arguing about objective/subjective experience and building religions around the life forms." That's the easy way out: worship the messenger, forget the message, pretend that you *get it.* And the drama plays on.

I can't admit that, can I, because you *prove it to me- ers* will slam this book shut and withdraw to your happy place, a rather large fortress barricaded by cynicism. More times than not we cue in on what we want to hear so that we can stop listening. Listening to anything beyond our assumptions is work and calls us into question. Can't have that!

The doe-eyed believers can't have that because it rubs against the grain of the blatant lies they live. The hardened cynics have had enough of the blatant lies and so they've divorced themselves from the doe-eyed believers. Now, anything that shares the same language as the believers sets off warning bells. If they'd listen with open ears instead of shutting off at the false alarm they'd be able to parse out fact from fiction. But these warning bells serve the same function as the blatant lies they caution against: To keep the brain from fully understanding Truth. To never move into 1st-person/I Am perspective. To remain self-centered and perhaps an arrogant elitist.

Cynicism Transcends Belief; Understanding Transcends All

Cynicism says, "I'm too smart to believe anything." Cool. But then arrogantly adds, "Therefore, there is nothing for which belief exists except misunderstanding and willful ignorance." Uncool.

Understanding, on the other hand, says, "I see that cynicism is another answer, which is truer than blind belief, but still unfulfilling. And, oh yeah, *arrogant.*"

The cynic hides. The believer hides. The messages fall on deaf ears or get corrupted by those whose ears are open only to what they want to hear.

Sometimes the messengers themselves fail because they couch what should be the purity of the message in preexisting religious terms. That failure is on purpose though. The purpose is to talk to the minority of folks who are ready to move beyond their religion in the religious language they comprehend. To the majority of witnesses a miraculous religious messenger appears and validates the truth claims of their religion. To the minority, Truth pierces the veil of their religion to say, "This ain't it. Come with me if you want to live!"

Or something less drastic but equally compelling.

What Understanding Is

Whelp, I've written the word *understanding* enough times now that I should probably define it in no uncertain terms. Understanding is seeing what is false thereby leaving the question of the true open.

Just because belief doesn't articulate Truth doesn't mean there is no Truth. And how will you find out if you don't grant yourself the freedom to ask without an answer already formulated?

Questions are freedom.

When you ask a guru type what the hell is wrong with the world and he strokes his beard and says, "Everything is as it should be," it makes you want to pull his beard out by the roots, right? What kind of answer is that? From the mouth of a poser it's nonsense and you're supposed to nod along. From the mouth of the one-eye open half asleep guy (as well as the enlightened) it's a true observation.

Everything is as it should be means that we are only ever acting from the available perspective. It sounds self-evident when you say it out loud but just try remembering it the next time you're in a fight with someone or your leader brings you to war. On the level that we live, war is still an issue. It's as it should be on this level. Understand this and snap out of the trance of the level. Suddenly you're no longer where your friends and family and president still are. When enough people snap out of it, a cultural sea change occurs and we adopt a whole new set of givens that we live in and wrongly call the highest.

Are we done with that game yet? Are you?

It's of no consequence to one who understands that everything is as it should be. Only the impeccability of his actions matter and that's why he never gets frustrated with you even when you want to yank his beard off and cause him pain.

Judgment Is Not Understanding

People connect with each other in different ways: intellectual, emotional, mutually self-serving, dysfunctional, cultural, religious—you know them; I don't need to recite them all. Now what is the relationship between one who understands this, lives life in understanding, and one who does not? Is it a one-way relationship? Is it compassion?

What it's not is judgment. Judgment is incompatible with compassion. Judgment is irrelevant to one who sees why people act the way they do. It doesn't mean a person's actions don't sometimes have negative consequences but that's for them to experience. The compassionate person may offer to point it out, illustrate the healthier alternative, but that's all one can do.

Judgment requires conversion. You need to sway people into believing you're righteous for your opinion to stick. The more people who believe what you believe the more affirmed and right and good and correct you feel. You feel safe. Comfortable. This is not compassion; it is arrogance. It is fortifying your baseless convictions. This is how we live our lives.

Calling it what it is isn't judging it. It's naming it. If hearing how you live your life makes it sound negative, perhaps that's because it is. Duh.

(*Duh* was a judgment, by the way.)

Condescending vs. Descending

Sounds like the compassionate person lives in a perpetual one-way relationship, doesn't it? Even if he can relate to you it becomes an act, like baby talking to toddlers.

Is that condescending? That's where judgment comes in and in this case is a healthy consideration: Is one condescending or just plain descending?

Is baby talking a baby a cold act? Parents talk with them on their own level. That's not an act of conceit or judgment. It's relating with Love.

Compassion and understanding are inseparable and they share a third component, which is Love. The

God-alive relate honestly to you with compassion, Love, and understanding, for such a one knows you as herself.

In Truth, there is no such thing as "I love you." There is only Love. There is the whole and the whole is Love.

Our "more enlightened" guru may descend from on high without condescending but he is still not penetrating your reality with the fullness of Love, for as we've already seen, the God-self aware are not trapped on the psycho-spiritual ladder extending itself higher and higher and infinitely higher through epochs of time. The "more enlightened" guru is trapped there just as you are and from both of your perspectives he is descending. From God's point of view, however, you both lack depth perception. You're only pretending there's a vertical continuum.

God-self awareness *is* the infinite and so may pierce the veil to relate with you at any moment in time, wherever you find yourself on those bars.

God-self awareness baby talks the "more enlightened" guru as well.

CHAPTER 14
Balance, Meditation, and The Integration of Self

You ever hear self-help gurus say in a calm Jedi voice that you need balance in your life? What do they mean by that? A balanced diet? Emotional balance? Inner ear? They use the term *balance* a lot because, generally speaking, we equate balance with health. What next spills out of their mouths are specific ideas culled from their interests or expertise. Like a hypnotized flock we are meant to take for granted that the specifications are correct.

Well, kindly allow me to introduce the meta-balance underlying the particulars few even know exists. This meta-balance is the proper arrangement of the free and fixed energy that comprise us. We have the ability to correctly organize the free and the fixed by simply being a blank slate, which means living in full awareness.

The goal of the body is to be as healthy as possible on all levels. When one quiets the mind the free energy aspect blossoms from within. In the absence of your will, the body performs necessary healthy actions. There is nothing to learn. There is no balance that you need to achieve. The body naturally maintains equilibrium when you step aside and let it speak its innate language.

The various practices spiritual gurus make money teaching are vestiges of what the body performs on its own when this operating system becomes the will of it. You, as an observing entity, still exist in this state, it's just that you're observing, you're aware, while the free flow works its magic.

You as observer, not actor: This is how the self is contextualized in the one-eye-open person. In that state of observing the body will always perform in proper proportion to its needs. Therefore, the perfect system for total health is no system. It is the relinquishing of ego. Even when the body movements seem nonsensical or perversely sexual they serve a purpose. You'll stick a finger in your rectum like a doctor administering a prostate exam if it means activating a chakra. There. I said it.

Now you know one reason why spiritual leaders keep secrets. Some unattractive things happen that serve the health of the body. These things come across as ludicrous when heard or read. Would you follow a spiritual leader who admitted he initially spent a lot of time with his hand up his butt? What if he said you might have to suffer the same? Kind of a turnoff isn't it?

Still, even the gross stuff is clinical in nature. Minor pain or discomfort may be involved in this consciousness revolution, depending on what the body needs, but nothing it can't handle. You may tap on your forehead with two fingers until it's raw, but if that's what's needed to open the so-called *third eye*, then go with the flow. Then again, you may not experience any of that. It really does depend on the needs of the individual body.

Another central justification for keeping this information hidden to all but a select few is that if the general public knew any of this we might think we had a choice in the matter. But let's revisit the butterfly analogy from Chapter 3. If the butterfly were to describe to the caterpillar how it has to become a sticky, gross pupa trapped in a cocoon in order to fly, the caterpillar might decide it's not worth the hassle. "Well, then I just won't fly. Forget it," she might say.

That's not really a choice, is it? Perhaps it is the butterfly's fault for not explaining this directly, but the fact is that the caterpillar transforms or it dies. The butterfly was most likely trying to sell the caterpillar on the miracle of flight as opposed to explaining the actual consequence of rejecting transformation: extinction.

Let this speaker be clear where others were not: We aren't having this discussion so that I can present an option to you. You have no choice unless you want humanity to fail. You can laugh at that, feel deep guilt, or however you process such a direct statement. When you're done wiggling you will stop and the cocoon will have become you. Wrapped in transformation thus, you will see that nothing you thought looked gross or ridiculous a minute ago is. The previous minute's interpretation came from the limited view of inexperience, immaturity. But here you are now in the experience. Not in it, you *are* it. You *are* the experience of transformation. You've got one eye open. Don't get stuck there or you'll never leave the cocoon.

***

I should add that if involuntary body movements sound suspiciously like horror movie demon possession, forget that noise. You can reassert your will anytime you want to stop the exercises. No devil takes over and you do trust it when it happens, for it is natural. Only as an afterthought does it feel unnatural. Because it's not your will moving the body, you want to ask, "Whose will is it?" But in the moment there is no question that these movements need to happen. Only with the interval of psychological time—with thought imposing its will on the brain—do you try to make the natural unnatural and enlightenment a fearful process.

All of this is to say that you will experience firsthand how you've abused the body by blocking out subtle energy for your own directives all these years. When one meditates, truly meditates, not forcing postures and rehearsed breathing techniques, the body is a temple, its action is prayer, and its surrounding environment is Heaven. It doesn't matter if that environment is a mountain, a church, a city apartment, a sewer, or hell.

All those guru books, magazines, and speeches that promote concentration and visualization as meditation are wrong. Meditation is the brain dissolving the self.

Leave thought behind. Be a blank slate. In this state of innocence energy flows freely.

Energy is its own director when you get out of the way; when you remain the director you steal its thunder. You contort energy for your own self-serving purpose. That is free will. That is the original choice from which all false choices arise. The self is an illusion and so every subsequent choice made by the self is an illusion.

Sick of redundancy yet?

I'll stop repeating myself when you do.

How The Body Knows What To Do

If it's a fact that the body just knows the right things to do to sustain its health and wake up psychically, how does it know? Where do these meditations and prayers and yogic postures come from? How does the body know to twirl in a circle, like a Whirling Dervish, or bless a room or assume the Crane Stance, Mr. Miyagi? How?

It knows because Truth informs it. Remember implicit order?

The body performs these natural acts of its own accord when it is living in a state of balance. There is no balance with you in charge, but when you step aside and become the passive observer, watch what Truth's action is. It's amazing!

To capture these performances and jot them down and repeat them consciously may gain you a result, but the result will never be Truth. It will be exercise. If you want to do exercises that's fine. Just don't fool yourself into believing you're on a higher plane or "on your way" to enlightenment. As noted, the only work one need do is dissolve long enough for energy to flow freely—but don't let the word *only* fool you, either. This is the hardest work on earth because it goes against everything you believe yourself to be. It goes against you. It's easy to reduce thought down to a single focal point and call that meditation. The challenge is to let go that final thought and with it, the thinker. *That* is real meditation and when that happens, all the physical and psychic exercises taught through industry occur spontaneously like instinct.

***

Say it with me, class: *One eye open is still half asleep.*

We all think we are different than our thoughts and emotions, but all we ever are is thought (from which sub-thoughts branch off.) The thinker is the culmination of senses trying to form a cohesive picture of the world by dividing and compartmentalizing experience. It turns experiencing into experiences; divides the ever-present now into past, present, future. The brain is the projector and you are the projected projecting evermore distantly through psychological time. Turn off the projector. Let go YOU.

Is it helpful that I'm telling you this?—No! Of course not! You still think you're the thinker separated from your thoughts. You still think there's a you owning and controlling thoughts. You're so self-absorbed no verbalization of Truth will remedy you.

Ouch!

If you're so hopelessly *you*, why are we having this discussion? It's because we need to be on the same page in order to turn it. Before we do that let's examine one more aspect of this blossoming: ascending and descending energy.

The Ups & Downs of Energy

Ever notice how it feels better to smile than to frown? Why?

Why do professional holy people smile so much—the gurus and yogis and lamas? Ever notice that?

Of course there are some who don't. Some professional holies make it a point to not smile or frown but remain emotionally neutral. What's all of this posturing for?

Smiling for smiling sake is produced by subtle energy ascending through the body. We are not referring to disorders like smile-mask syndrome or Angelman syndrome. We're talking about the smile of spiritual equilibrium. Hearing this you may start smiling to create the ascent of energy. You may write books on how to smile properly—the pros and cons of smiling. What do biologists say about smiling? How do priests weigh in on this?—the whole rigmarole.

Smiling that is produced by ascending energy and not, say, a fart joke, cannot be cultivated by you. But that won't stop many of you from trying. As we know, humans will do anything to remain in control. We'll claim ascending energy is active in us already and as proof, look at me! I'm smiling!

But that's fakery. Repression is not joy. Accept no substitutes.

The ascent and descent of subtle energy is just body mechanics, really. Up/down, ascend/descend, mean nothing more than etheric current flow in the body. Energy works the body and informs action. In the case of descending energy, it can become trapped in the body in the form of emotions. It can manifest as disease, cancer, depression, all the horrible outcomes of the separate self.

Etheric energy's ability—Truth's ability—to manifest and move in the body is equal to the amount of self you are willing to give up. Give up partially and experience Truth as an interpenetrating force. Give up entirely and you are Truth self-aware. No more ascending/descending, for the body is totally submersed. This stasis is where the next revelation lives: all of that ascending/descending movement is, like everything you do, a trick to placate your desire to seek higher consciousness and therefore sustain you.

Discoveries like ascending/descending energy often make the person floating along an inner path to enlightenment feel as though they've arrived someplace significant. This feeling is natural when you live in relationship to, not as, Truth.

Your penultimate fear is nonattachment. It is the last thing you want no matter how much you protest out loud or in silence because it is annihilation in disguise. So, to those stoic monks who never smile, who think they must create a balance in energy—never happy, never sad, total equilibrium—we say: Welcome to Planet Bland. You're still controlling, dominating, and directing. Let go. What mandate exists?

And to the New Age woo-woo crowd let it be known that we see right through you too. Wide eyes soak in external light to compensate for the darkness inside. Stop.

It's time to grow up now.

CHAPTER 15
What Is Love?

Love. One of a handful of words we use confidently every day while privately wondering at its meaning. Kind of insane when you think about it. It's as if we're robots programmed to ask questions a certain way to achieve an answer and if we never get that answer we just keep asking over and over again for all eternity. It rarely occurs to us that we're asking the question wrongly. The question isn't, "What is Love?" The question is, "What isn't Love?"

To see what Love is you must acknowledge what Love is not. Seeing what Love is not means dropping your projections. Once dropped, if Love is real, it is there. So ask, *What isn't Love?*

Love is not jealousy, hatred, lust, abuse, self-content, fleeting happiness, anger, or any of the other emotional states and responses we attach to that word. Where Love is—true Love—these other things are not. And where these other things are, Love is blocked out. Not totally, though. It pierces through as much as one allows, usually just enough for you to turn it into a craving for more and then seek it. Look, we're not the smartest species alive, okay, just the smartest on the planet. There are billions of planets!

The self embraces craving not Love. It filters this tiny morsel of a feeling into all of its conditional responses. It loves Love but loves itself more. It won't tell you this; that is, you will never admit this to yourself, but this is the fact that predicts you.

Love Is Indivisible

Is it overly cynical to say there's no such thing as true Love between couples, or is it a fact? Are there happy couples out there that love each other beyond the initial romance phase, or are they merely people who feel lonely and are comfortable working on their personal dysfunctions with a partner?

Is there anything wrong with settling down? With raising a family? How else does human life propagate?

Where does this Love with a capital L reside?

So many questions!

One thing is for sure: It's easier to settle down than put these questions to ourselves. If we knew how to love, coupling would not be an issue. Absolute Love does not choose one over another. Relative love does. Perhaps that's why we call them relatives.

Trust Love, End The Journey

You have infinite depths to explore if you can swim beyond the sandbar. Of course plunging the depths sucks. It's hard work, there's constant pressure on all sides, and although the creatures lurking about diminish in number, they are larger and more grotesque. You are a menace to yourself, but let go. Take the plunge. All of that is a description of the hero's journey. It can take forever or be instantaneous; it's all in how you struggle, so stop struggling. Every marriage is a marriage of convenience for those who plod.

What's that you say? The shallow end of the ocean is overpopulated and the depths too lonely?

Actually, the shallow end is overpopulated and so we will either stagnate and die or commit persona suicide—the big leap of faith—and leave mortality behind. Both choices are death but only one leads to hell. Hell is where we are right now. Over and over again, right now. The other looks like hell to us but that's because we are so accustomed to our cage that freedom looks evil.

Christians wonder why evil can never understand the greatness of God's plan. That is only ever a metaphor for you. You are God rotting in the hell you create and calling it *life* or *mediocrity* or *subjective experience.*

Billions of fear-filled subjective views blend together to form one angry, hateful scene.

Wake up! Of course the depths of you are lonely and scared. And him and her and everyone. Billions of people living side by side, lonely and scared. Some admit it; some don't. All suffer. I would do the Gen-X thing here and point out the irony but it's time to stop hiding in snarkiness.

True humor is born of innocence. We've perverted it into an emotional shield, which is necessary up to a point. This is that point. Beyond this point all shields must fall.

Take the plunge. Take it. And don't hold your breath for the water is also you. If you see that, then the journey is over. There are no shallows and depths from the point of view of the ocean itself and it is this viewpoint the brain adopts when it leaves you at the altar.

It is the holding your breath, the latching onto that one final separation, that creates fear, pain, and loneliness. As the doctor tells the laboring mother, "Just breathe."

The brain must choose: your will or Love. One road leads to frustration and the hell you construct; the other to nirvana. Actually, the other isn't a road at all. It's as if you've come to a nonsensical fork. Path #1 seems to stretch on forever in new and winding directions. Path #2 just ends. It's a dead end. There is no road there. As a traveler searching for enlightenment you inevitably choose Path #1. On you go, some would say, in ignorance of your mistake. But it isn't your mistake; it's the brain's, right? The mistake happens by design. You're a mere pawn in a game the brain is playing to remain in control because it fears the unknown.

I'm No Guide Either

We are having this discussion not because I want to guide you but because we must sterilize all that has come before and, indeed, all that you claim to be. I am not teaching you anything with a practical use. You can turn it into that if you want, but we are so over self-help and comparative studies as a species that turning this into either would be more than a perversion, it would be a fatal error.

So I'm not a teacher even if you're learning new things. This isn't knowledge for you to accumulate; it's meant to shut you up. What's important is that the brain stops its activity for the new operating system to kick in. Think of it this way: If I can give you all of these real answers to the questions you assumed were big unanswerable ones, imagine the depth of the new set of questions awaiting on the other side of resolution.

When your vision of your world is altered and narrowed down to just this one thing, just the wrecking ball that is these words, it is easier to let go. This book is your final illusion. Let it destroy you then you it. Then you will know free will. Then you will be Love.

I don't blame you if you're skeptical of all this Love business. If I were you I'd be asking, "Uuuuuh, dude? We're all asleep and dreaming, right? So if the dream comes from Love why does it feel like a nightmare? I know what you'll say, you'll say, *The nightmare is you.* But, like, why am I the nightmare? Why the separation between this black-and-white Truth and the spiritual hierarchy's shades of gray? Can't Love just come here and wipe away the pain and confusion and separations?"

And if I were me, I'd answer, "Yes. But then what would we have to talk about?" If I were Truth I'd be cleverer and say, "All things must be expressed including you waking up from the self-perpetuated nightmare."

Here's the deal: God is the eternal process whose entire thrust is Love. The process appears to flow from creator to creation and, if humanity gets its act together, back to creator. But when that circuit happens even its veil falls to reveal the entire process itself emanating from formless intelligence. Everything, everything, everything is formless intelligence pulsating, radiating, playing in and as Love. It fully reveals itself, fully expresses itself, as it choicelessly must.

Humanity is a form that has the ability to express the self-awareness of the formless intelligence radiating it. If God's process flows creator to creation, then humanity's process flows backwards from creation to creator. We close the loop and the last veil falls.

When we abandon the brain-projected self, God-self fills us and our creative process also becomes one of Love. Unfortunately, humanity lives in the self-constructed slum called *myself* and so does not acknowledge any of this. Humanity lives in sickness. What is sick heals or dies. It is that elementary.

CHAPTER 16
Positive Negation

For thousands of years respected people like Lao Tzu said, "Seek the path of Truth" or words to that effect. Many moons later Jiddu Krishnamurti comes along and says, "Do not seek. There is no path. Truth is a pathless land." Which is correct?

It's a trick question and you'll be forgiven for expecting me to answer with, "Do not seek." For once I'm not going to. Instead, I'm going to say, "Those who said 'seek' didn't mean it," and then I won't have to say not to.

This is another example of how language is a barrier to Truth. When Lao Tzu or Buddha or any Christ comes along and says, "Seek," they don't mean, "Look for Truth." They mean, "Look. Truth is right here. There's nothing to look for; there's only looking." Or more succinctly, "Look. Truth *is*."

Look how?

Not with the eyes. Not by choosing a way. Be still and sight happens.

When Krishnamurti said, "Do not seek," he didn't mean that you should repress your desire to seek. The other enlightened folk didn't mean that we should actively seek and Krishnamurti didn't mean the opposite. All meant, "Be still," or simply, "Be."

That's frustrating to active creatures like us. We assume there must be something we can do to facilitate this whole other understanding we've been talking about. How does one look if not with the outer eyes of body or the inner eye of contemplation? How can we be still?

That's where positive negation comes in.

Truth is met through negation. Where untruths are Truth is not. That's self-evident, right? So we must negate all of the answers we've built up about Truth. We can't negate them with more answers in mind. In other words, we can't negate in order to prove a hypothesis. We cannot expect a result from negating. Expectation is more of our own activity and when done right, positive negation stops our activity, which is why it's such a powerful tool.

Pealing away answers is like pealing an onion: There is no center, just layer upon interconnected layer. When there's nothing left, the power of the question remains. This deconstruction works not only for universal topics but personal ones as well. (For more on that, please see Chapter 10.)

The Power of No Intention

Positive negation stops the activity of thought by stripping away all that we've conjured about Truth or Love or any unknowable. It eliminates our logical database and our basic assumptions. Normally when we take away it is with the intent to replace or upgrade. Really, really crudely speaking, we use the right hemisphere of our brain to sift the universal information field for answers that we then make sense of and store in the left hemisphere for later use. Well, with positive negation we've stripped away the answers of the left hemisphere with no intention of searching for more answers using the right hemisphere. In that stopped moment, in a lightning flash, Truth happens.

Truth is living, vital. Once you see that all of the answers emanating from you are not Truth, Truth acts. Truth bursts through that dam and pours forth the flood. Behind the hyperbole lies a real spiritual event that happens in the body: activation of the universal power source. Scholars and critics often miss this fact.

The negation thing sounds backwards because we tend to see evil as negative and good as positive and in a way we're saying that absolute good cannot be lived through positive means.

In Truth, the negative *is* the positive. It is the key to the door of the positive. What we call evil is the avoidance of this fact and of claiming responsibility for one's actions. Evil *is* one's actions when one lives as an ego self. Christians call this *Original Sin*; Hindus call it *karma*. You will call it anything to avoid turning that key because there is no room for the ego beyond the door to enlightenment. Since you are that ego, stepping through the door is suicide of the mind. The mind will avoid this at all costs.

Think of yourself as a virus. The remedy is to invade the logical answer-seeking brain by negating all its answers. Beat it at its own game. Tear down its walls. With nowhere to run, the brain is quiet. It is only when you are quiet that another may be heard. So sayeth the analogy.

CHAPTER 17
No Such Thing As Progress

To give you an idea how ridiculous a species we are, let's say we're energy and logic. Put another way, we're fire and the wheel. Thousands of years of discovery and we've not moved beyond fire and the wheel! See how ridiculous that is?

Most notions of progress are.

That sounds cynical if you believe in, say, social progress, but is there such a thing?

Is there not only ever a war of conflicting ideas, the outcome of which becomes prevailing thought? Resistance to the prevailing thought builds and there is another war. This grinding together of memes can birth more freedom or more repression. This is not confined to social advancement; it's true for everything from politics to scientific discovery to invention. The car, for example, gives one more freedom to move about. However, the car owner is a slave to industry and law. Laws are necessary to keep brain-selves disciplined. God-self lives rightly; morality and ethics flow naturally through all of one's actions.

Hold on. Don't let me get away with this. Question it: Even if the car owner is beholden to industry the fact of the car is a giant leap from the fact of the pull cart. Is that not progress? It is within a limited frame just as civil rights law is progress within a limited frame.

Increasingly our world is purposely eroding its freedoms because it fears losing them. That is a fact. This is not just happening in America, it's happening across the globe. Now, that fact doesn't make sense does it? Taking away freedom to preserve freedom? Isolated, it sounds totally illogical so we must shift perspectives if we are to find the reason for it.

Doors are closing on our world. It is a human hand that shuts them. We're depleting our natural resources, overpopulating our lands, and none of that progress we believe we're making has satiated desire. Neither have the entertainments and addictions we've hooked ourselves on. The wealthiest nations have access to all manner of information and sensation to quench desire but none of it amounts to anything in the end. These are such obvious facts now that some of you feel like you're reading a tired cliché.

When did killing the earth to kill ourselves become passé? How has it come to this?

Here is the hard fact about progress: In the grand scheme of things progress is only ever a short-term gain. We swing back and forth, progress and regress, on a pendulum motored by social forces. This is because we don't always agree on what constitutes progress and even when we do, those in power who have a selfish interest in preserving the status quo or rolling back progress wield their pens and swords.

What long-term good are rights and medical breakthroughs when all it takes is the press of a button to annihilate everyone?

We're depleting Earth of the very things we need to survive because we're divorced from our survival drive. We're married to desire as a drive. What do you think will result from a species that is so out of touch with their physical environment that they'd sacrifice it to appease the wants of their mental addictions?

None of this even begins to address the question of "Progress for whom?" Is destroying indigenous populations in the name of expansion and consumerism for a dominating culture progress? Is child labor as a cost-cutting measure progress? What about privatized prison systems and medicine as growth industries? What about war?

Are further social equalities advancements if they are used to satiate the masses so they will turn a blind eye to atrocities committed in the name of those advancements? Have the filthy rich allowed us to be comfortable enough that we don't pay attention to their pillaging other nations? Are technological strides worth patting ourselves on the back for today if there will be no one left to enjoy them tomorrow?

Social and to a slightly lesser extent technological progress aren't born from a place of malice. Martin Luther King, Jr. didn't wake up one day and say, "I have a dream... to create a nation of racial equality so that together we can all ignore global injustices committed in our names." Search as you might you will never find a speech from The Wright Brothers declaring, "Let this flying wing evolve into a weapons-carrying war machine. Together with the state we will build a mighty air force!"

Of course those are not the origins of great strides. Innocence is. The struggle for freedom over the physical and political landscape is. But our lowest impulses bastardize inventions. Inevitably.

Politically, when a great upheaval settles, dominant elites manipulate the new context they find society in so that they can remain dominant elites. And they can only do that with our approval. Self-appointed leaders foster loud, cheering approval to overcompensate for the crime of being self-appointed. Democratically elected leaders may garner that but more often than not they are met with calm approval.

The same holds true for technological strides. When the cheering settles, that which can be turned into a weapon will be. Dictators are overt egomaniacs so they roll out their death toys to great propagandistic fanfare to illustrate their dominance. Democratically elected leaders hide this progress beneath the words "Top Secret."

The hunter's instinct that obsessively creates such toys is the dilemma, not the demeanor of the regimes who manage them.

Desire & The Fallacy of Spiritual Advancement

Many assume the core of the problem is that humankind has advanced socially and technologically, but we've not kept pace spiritually. This view maintains that if we forge on as an unbalanced species we will eventually destroy ourselves.

This is not true.

Brain-selves are not spiritually unbalanced; they are cut off from Spirit-self awareness. Spirit isn't out of balance; it's missing. God-self awareness is either present in the body or it is not. There is no spiritual evolution prior to it for it affects real evolution. The aspect of us keeping pace with social and scientific advances is not Spirit but desire.

Desire is the weed that kills us.

Desire is want. The root of want is the repression of Godhead and all its psychic accessories. This repression creates lust for power. It's the same old problem: We need to transcend self for God-self. We don't want to. We opt to turn ourselves into God. We suffocate our senses in entertainment, drugs, sex, shopping, religion, personal drama—whatever our particular vices are that heighten emotional and physical sensation.

We likewise drown ourselves in information. We have knowledge and sensation on demand. We are creating artificial intelligence that will serve us. Everything we do is to preserve us, serve us, protect us, and worship us. How is that going for us?

Even with these vast stores of knowledge and sensations at our fingertips we are miserable. Nothing any of us are doing will dissolve this misery. We feel pointless, aimless, and we'll be homeless if we continue our scorched earth policy. On the whole we're too depressed or too preoccupied to fix the problem. Because we don't live the God viewpoint we crave it above all else even as we suppress it. Feeding this insatiable appetite will be the death of our species.

We are our own executioners. We kill freedom so that freedom may flourish. That is totally illogical by itself and yet it's exactly what is happening, so we know that it isn't happening in a vacuum. It's happening as a result of something. It is the logical prelude to the final clash every woken species on the brink of its next evolutionary leap faces: suicidal impulse vs. survival instinct.

None of this has to happen. If you wake up right now this all vanishes, for this is the stuff of time. It is a grand inevitable consequence to not waking up, not stepping out of psychological time.

The ending of a time cycle is a rush. It's like being forced through the birth canal: we will be born anew or we will miscarry. And so what are a few thousand years of progress worth if they are wiped out with near extinction and the amnesia that follows?

Is that really happening? Is humanity unfolding in a bubble that either reveals itself as a spiral or remains a closed loop when it pops? Is that whole movement not true linear time?

Attachment & Power

Let's go back to desire for a sec. Most say desire is about attachment and leave it at that. That's unfortunate because there is more. Attachment isn't the root. Lust for attachment is derived from the lust for power, but before we get into it, what do we mean by the word *attachment*? Doesn't it usually have something to do with owning objects and using something or someone as a crutch? Isn't that movement of cheating, owning, and controlling brought about by the lust for more power?

And what is power? Generally speaking, power is freedom beyond the common man. That's what the hoarding of wealth is for right? Access. Movement. Control.

What is power beyond those freedoms? What is it to someone who has everything?

The ultimate political power is conversion. It's steering the herd toward your vision but always keeping them under you, never as equals. There is no power in equality. Ultimate power is having the victim identify with you and in that identification, understand that you are the authority figure. This is how the state works. This is how cults work. This is foreign policy. It's Stockholm syndrome.

Even though this world we've created is an illusion, you live in it and it affects you and you want to know what the people in power think they are achieving. They are simply addicted to their own lies and have lots of money and subordinates to hide their addiction.

That's not a satisfying answer is it? Not if you're politically savvy.

If you're an angry educated observer you know that capitalism rules the day. The U.S. houses 5% of the world's population, yet produces 72% of all hazardous waste and consumes 33% of the world's paper. Capitalism is spreading globally from under the umbrella corporation that is the American Empire. In accordance, 2nd and 3rd-World nations must feed the beast. Their lands become dumping grounds contaminated with factories and oil pumps ruled by puppet dictator to the atrocities of whom we turn a blind eye.

Third World people are ants for the crushing. Second World people have chain restaurants and retail outlets and feel like they're "coming up." The top one percent of the First World dominates everything. That is the system. That is what's going on. And that failure is the best-case scenario for rampant capitalism.

Abysmal, isn't it? Oh, but it could be worse. A lot worse.

Capitalism gets worse *if it works*. The ideal is that First World nations spread their wealth and the globe becomes one of economic equality. This is statistically unfeasible. What happens when every country increases its hazardous waste output a thousand-fold and eats up the remaining trees? The failed system is a slow death; the morally and ethically correct system is an instantaneous extinction.

So what do we do? Abandon Capitalism? For what? What works? Oh the anxiety! The depression!

The horror... the horror....

Look, trading one system for another won't matter in the long term. No outward movement will. There is one answer from which all others fall into place: You as living, breathing Truth is that answer. This is the only way. You can be this right now.

You must.

You Can't Binge & Purge Desire

There is a school of thought that says we should indulge all desires until we no longer desire. Appealing though that may sound, the caged gerbil rarely tires of running in its wheel. It may stop for a while to rest, but it always climbs back in.

Choosing a path means choosing an outcome. Those on a path to Truth project the outcome. The desire for Truth creates the achievement of it, but it's not really achievement. It's a self-fulfilled prophesy. Those people who self-fulfill will either rest there and call that Truth and blindly carry on living their lives in false piety or they will grow restless, realizing that what they thought was the final answer wasn't, and move on from there. This is the cycle that predicts them, like the gerbil going nowhere fast.

And once again we're confronted with the firm fact that you can't even ask, "How do we achieve enlightenment? How do we get off the wheel?"

There is no how. There is no achieving.

Seeing the falseness in how we act, understanding deeply and not just intellectually, not just agreeing because it looks factually the case, is the end-all-be-all non-action that is required to step out of time. It's not an action or a *how* that can be triggered by you. It's that when the brain sees the fact that it cannot affect a change or find Truth, it rests. It stops projecting you.

You, the defense mechanism.

You, the seeker.

Vanished.

Truth flowers in that open space that formerly was you. Since you have vanished, psychological time has vanished. The body remains in physical time and Truth instructs it from the timeless state. That alone is balance.

CHAPTER 18
Another Recap That Moves Us Forward

You are the dam that holds back the ocean. When the brain understands this epiphany deeply, in all quadrants of itself, not merely logically, the epiphany bulldozes the dam, the *you*. In rushes Truth with its implicit order.

Again we caution not to get tangled in words. Words are an approximation of the thing described and the thing described lives in nonverbal non-action. When spiritual leaders say one cannot talk about Truth that is what they mean. They don't mean that Truth can't be articulated, but that the articulation is its death and the hearer will use the carcass as her plaything. The verbalization of Truth becomes the fundamentalism of tomorrow because the depths the words were meant to convey can only be lived. To not live Truth is to talk about it, discard it, build a system upon it, make holy objects to represent it, debate it, collapse it—anything but live it.

It's a big ol' paradox, right? To speak Truth is to bring it into the time stream thereby killing it. Humans exist in this time stream so we have no choice but to speak it. Since Truth is God-self awareness acting through organisms and we organisms block it out, arguably we're the ones who are dead. It makes sense that we'd kill Truth. Inevitably, we want to warp it into a thing of the time stream because that's where we exist. That's who we are and so even if Truth says, "Stop being who you are," we accept or reject that—yet either action is a means of remaining who we are because our impulse is to do something about it. If you do anything about it, the action becomes another layer of who you are.

God loves irony, what can I tell you?

When it comes to Truth, translation is a wrong action. In trying to understand what Truth says we naturally make the words fit our patterns, our sense of what is acceptable. What is acceptable is lorded over by the self and so it will always be wrong—*always!*—for that which is not Truth is falsehood.

Quite the conundrum for the enlightened guy who wants to teach the world, eh?

It would be, except we noted that the enlightened cannot teach; one can only point out. It appears to be a fine-line distinction, but such a one is not judging you, which involves giving advice or rules. One is explaining what is and now you're cursed with the knowledge. What you do with it is your problem. Enlightened folks are jerks that way.

The moment you wake up you see the falseness of the pupil/master dichotomy. There is no dichotomy. One is poking oneself with a hot iron through you, that's all.

You also see that you weren't spiritually unbalanced. You were in a spiritual coma hence the term *asleep*. The body moved through space-time devoid of God-self awareness. You built and destroyed societies, ripped apart ecosystems, and stood on the crushed lives of others for the high. You were an ignorant, needy child beast playing in the dark and demanding more toys. You flailed about, threw things and broke things. You cried a bunch. You felt bad. You turned that emotion into resolve and carried on differently in many ways but the same where it counts. Your life of control was out of control.

You see all of that quite clearly when the light comes on. In that moment, you see that there are no laws to contain the beast. There is no advice that modifies our behavior forever because we are the problem. When you live on a pendulum, you swing.

In fact, here's the only advice I will give you, author to reader: Put this book down and forget you ever read it. Abandon all that you've absorbed here.

Forget you ever were.

CHAPTER 19
Is God Creating A Partner?

There is nothing real in the way we live our lives. When we say drastic things like, "Life is an illusion," that doesn't mean we're not alive, it means we're living wrongly. Wrongly in that we concentrate on what we sense physically and interpret emotionally, kind of like how your eyes are sensing these words and making you depressed! (Heh. Sorry.)

Materialism is another form of fundamentalism. Materialists therefore miss the point entirely that physicality is energy. There's no rigid particle/wave duality. There is energy in various states of itself. This energy is consciousness. It is God. It is Truth.

Living in separation as we do we nonetheless feel some semblance of oneness. We feel our core but don't recognize it for what it is so we attach it to some separate thing: the sun, the dollar, a text, a chant, an animal, an alien race, nature, music, whatever. Then we worship this separate thing or live in relationship with it. Fear is naturally involved because beneath the surface we know this is wrong.

There is no contradiction in any of it. It's flavors in the same recipe for disaster. Why concentrate on wisdom old or new when the end result is disaster? For how many generations do you think we can live wrongly without exterminating ourselves? For how many more generations can we put off 1st-person God-self awareness for worship or relationship?

All is God. The exterminator is only ever one cutting off one's leg to save the body. There is pain but a new leg grows in its place. If that new leg also goes numb, it gets chopped off and the cycle continues. It is brutal if you let it be.

Actually, calm down. We're not really the leg. If the purpose in all of this is to make the physical universe God-self aware, then we are the fingernails or the hair, not the leg. We're this thriving dead thing, a living contradiction.

We're zombies! Cool!

But zombies with an agenda. An agenda to find the light and nourishment that only Truth provides so that we can stop groping around in the dark muttering, "Brains!"

We zombies idealize the end to suffering. Then we seek it. Then we never find it. Why? Because we're zombies! We *are* the state of suffering! To lose that is to lose the self. Thankfully, some do lose themselves. Others are contented to explain what this means without experiencing it. Does that make a whit of sense?

Some sideline observers claim the real reason we transform is because God is waking the physical universe to create an equal partner. This would be a counterpart not separate but symbiotic, a true wave/particle relationship. Such a notion begs the question: Could that partner divide itself from the wave like a cell splitting? Is that what life is driving toward?

Yes and no. That happens but only on another illusory level. Recall that ultimately energy is the result of No-Thing bearing a necessary quality: intelligence. Wait, *bearing* is the wrong word; *being* is more like it. No-Thing *is* intelligence. The *No* of No-Thing is the formless self-aware aspect of it.

Formless intelligence is indivisible on its own terms. Only through creation can it experience divisions. Creation is a necessary illusion and in that illusion partnerships may be forged. Like everything else it is both real and unreal. Necessity is the root of this paradox. Remaining on the sideline is the root of intellectualizing wrongly. All of that said, I won't roll my eyes if you're still wondering how the awakened brain affects the universe.

The original intention of memory is survival. Something that is rotten smells rotten and you know not to eat it. Fire burns and so on. The body's survival depends on sensory memory.

Seeing fire reminds you of being burned. If you're an animal you stay away from it. With humans comes the unique ability to translate, use metaphor, assign meaning, and so forth, so if you're a human you stay away from it and you assign a moral quality to it: Fire bad! (Or you worship it: Fire is God! Or you invent a God that will "bring" you fire.)

The living of oneness takes place at the subatomic level. Your realizing oneness by dissolving rigid false conclusions is the same as saying the particle realizes formlessness through giving over to the force of its wave aspect. Waveform is the creator/partner of particle form. That is the physical correlate to the mental waking. Nothingness shines through you. The fabric of the universe, which you are, "gains" that much more sentience, that much more transcendental awareness. Individual awakening does not merely affect everything, it is everything.

Still, let's not forget the paradox: she who makes waking her goal does not understand what she is reading.

And let's also not forget that God is not creating a partner but expressing its self-awareness through its numerous separate bodies.

CHAPTER 20
Physics & Understanding

Aaaaaah, finally. We've made it to physics. See?—I told ya we'd deal with this later. It's later. And I've got a heaping dish of pseudoscience leftovers from Chapter 11. Where to being, where to begin?

Hey, remember when scientists believed in spontaneous regeneration? They saw maggots wriggling in rotten meat and figured the little wormy fellers emerged spontaneously from it. Nowadays people go, "Duh! Of course flies lay eggs in the meat, stupid."

What's stupid now was smart then, for there was a day when spontaneous regeneration did not sound ludicrous. That day is today.

Go to your dictionary and look up *force*. By the quantum physics definition, it is intrinsic direction woven into the fabric of reality. That's where the definition ends: intrinsic action of the universe. Direction without a director. Spontaneous direction. Does that not sound strikingly like the same blindness as spontaneous regeneration?

It is absurd to believe that there is pressure or direction being applied to something without anything applying it. This would be a real miracle and science doesn't believe in those. The problem is that physics only goes as far as it can prove. It may theorize beyond its proven boundaries but the boundaries remain until rendered moot by repeatable testing or better math.

Theoretical quantum physics has an impact on the rest of the hard sciences as well as religion. There are those who say God will be discovered through quantum physics. There are whole sects of Eastern religions who have attached themselves to this hope. They find a link between spiritual oneness and quantum mechanics, which seems to illustrate the oneness of the physical universe. The link is tenuous, however, because for the physicist quantifiable fact ends at force.

Science has its roots in observation and understanding. The great scientists have a passion for understanding. Now they've hit this wall, which is the fact that there is an underlying fabric or oneness to the universe. This is as far as the physicist can go if she is living as a separate entity. The part may recognize the whole logically but it can't go the distance without taking that next step: being the whole. Put another way, the wave must crash back into the ocean to see that it was ocean all along.

So the physicist is stuck at force and she can experiment all she wants with parallel universes, dark matter, antimatter, all that fun stuff—yet she will not touch force. Since she has a passion to understand, why can't she see the problem?

In this case, as with enlightenment, the passion to understand brings one to the brink of direct perception but then it gets in the way. The logical framework impedes breakthrough. Breakthrough requires 1st-person experience, not 3rd-person objectification, so while it is true that logic can bring you to force's door, kindly leave it at the door.

To understand what force is one must be enlightened because force is implicit instruction for the subatomic world. It is Truth for physics. This can't be proven scientifically but it can be known through the perceptual shift enlightenment creates.

Logic is neither the key to all doors nor the lamp that illuminates the interiors beyond. By saying, "Okay, I'll experiment with this. This book has a theory that if I stop thinking something amazing will take place. I'll test it to find out," you create a motive and are back to seeking.

If allowed, the larger thrust of quantum physics will be to arrive at the point where every logical conclusion has been drawn and still the scientist is left scratching her head, saying, "I don't know." Not "I still don't know," which implies that she will know.

When all unknowns become known and you still don't know, that's a good indication you've got something unknowable on your hands. (You're welcome.) Saying you will know the unknowable means you will keep giving yourself false answers derived from the known. There's still a search going on and the implication is that you have an answer waiting to be realized. Now we're back to self-fulfilling prophesy.

The larger thrust of physics must end in "I don't know." Logic has done its best. Its best is a dead end. So you sigh and sit and do nothing for nothing is all that can be done. The best movement in your repertoire has run its course. All that is left is no movement. In that instance, psychological time stops. There is no time and so there is no object in time. The self is gone. The scientist is gone. The seeker is gone, right? A seeker sitting still isn't seeking and thus is a seeker no more.

The revolution is instantaneous. Only in the quiet mind is the universe revealed for all things spring eternal in nothing. And here we are again at that central point: Don't seek, BE. There simply is not another way. Abandon logic all ye who enter here.

The Observer Effect – Layer 1

Physicists believe that thought influences subatomic particles. As if by magic, particles behave according to the observer's expectations. They don't know why that happens so let's give them a helping hand....

All subatomic structures have apparent particle/wave duality. The information contained in these structures is in superposition. Superposition is the point where all probable outcomes for the wave/particle intersect. It's like virtual memory that exists equally in either wave or particle state.

But hold up. What are these subatomic structures in the first place? I mean what is a particle anyway?

It's electromagnetic radiation. Subatomic particles are light expressed in a variety of wavelengths.

Light. Light? Let there be light? That's the bed of energy in which everything manifests? Maybe the Jews were onto something, but let's not get ahead of ourselves here.

Let's go back to the original question: How does thought influence subatomic particles? The answer is that light is light whether in the particle or the wave state, but the fluidity of the wave state is what allows information from other sources—in this case, thought— to inform its actions. One could say the wave is the particle listening.

How that happens is this: Everything is energy disguised as separate things, so even that wave/particle duality is a disguise. The wave is not a structure unto its own. Much like an ocean wave is no different than the ocean it plays in, the one energy is similarly disguised. That's where the ocean/energy metaphor ceases being useful because an ocean really is a thing. It exists in time. It takes time for information to travel from one end of the ocean to the other.

Energy is timeless and endless; hence information does not travel on it. Information penetrates it instantaneously. Thought, as brain waves, directly informs and overrides the natural function of a subatomic particle by activating one of its probabilities in superposition. Not just any probability: it activates the one that you are thinking of and expecting—the one that your thought wave *is*. One could say that the observer possesses and controls the particle.

Hey! Not unlike when brain-self awareness gives over to God-self awareness!

Easy there, Poindexter. We're moving on.

Emptiness—the *No* of No-Thing—is the ultimate non-state prior to yet inclusive of all states. We cannot detect absolute nothing by observation; we can only detect *things*. The deeper we dig the more we find.

The Observer Effect – Layer 2

The next big discovery in physics will be that particles don't just respond to thought they are created by it. If the physicist digs deeply enough she will eventually be shoveling dirt created by her own thought. She may see that dirt responds to her expectations and deduce that this deeper layer is the same as the previous. Therefore, her final answer is that thought influences reality.

Regrettably, she is mistaken.

She's not taking into account that she passed the ground of all matter and is now sculpting out of her own subjective layer of clay. That which she is projecting appears to respond only to her—but she is the projector so what she's projecting *is her.*

There are two layers to what we're describing. Layer one is thought influencing particles. Layer two acts like layer one so it's harder to detect but it is distinct. Layer two is particles created by the act of observing nothingness. Nothingness is impossible to observe; therefore, the very trying creates more particles. This is dangerous knowledge if it's possible to influence matter in a way that subverts the laws of physics. And it is....

Lucid Waking

Have you ever become conscious that you were dreaming while you were dreaming? Have you ever woken up inside the dream and taken conscious control of your actions? These are facets of what's known as *lucid dreaming* and you must do the reverse here: wake your dream-state consciousness into the wake-state self. Merge the two. Merge the conscious with the unconscious. One who is undivided in such a way has the power to subvert the laws of physics. That's *lucid waking.*

But how to go about this, hmm? Oh, it's as easy as anything else in this book—You do it by accessing the speed faster than light. Yes, there is a speed faster than light: the speed of relationship.

The speed of relationship is faster than the speed of light for it is a simultaneous interaction between observer and observed. Relationship between particles and conscious intent must have always already existed prior to physicists having discovered the relationship.

The speed of light needn't be broken to travel the universe. For that, we need to understand the nature of relationship as cause/effect, not cause and then effect. There is no time lapse involved, just the appearance of one. Explore that fact and everything will change.

Actually, why wait? Let us explore it now.

Cause and effect are actually cause/effect. It happens simultaneously as a stream. The time lapse between the observer and the observed takes place on the surface level. At the subatomic level, all cause/effect is simultaneous but it may take time for the effect to bubble up to the surface of the observer's awareness. If, however, the observer's consciousness is undivided she does not experience a lapse in time. Such a person knows cause/effect as the very inseparable stream that she is.

If your head hasn't exploded yet, you may be wondering if people with undivided minds ever use that power to control reality. The answer is *no.* Only in the nightmare of separation do you imagine an amoral "complete" person, a devil, or an evil superman.

At the highest level of consciousness, a being can still give up enlightenment. Lust can creep back in at that highest level—further evidence that the consciousness ladder is truly monkey bars—but not at the level beyond levels. Lust and greed have no relationship to one who has stepped out of the game. Whole people are not sociopaths.

If the person who has stepped outside the game wants to interact with people trapped in the hierarchy, then lust, for example, would be a conscious act. It would be acting. Such a one assumes a role and plays it out like Yoda pretending to be a swamp simpleton or Mr. Miagi pretending to be from Los Angeles. However, there are limits to the act. This person could not murder or cause wars. An enlightened person cannot be anti-life as an actor. Someone should have told Yoda that.

Singularity

The fall is an act of God. The forgiveness is an act of God. The reconciliation and ascension are acts of God. All is God including the ability to imagine otherwise. Including the ability to deny this and act according to one's own lies.

All of human evolution has led us to this point. When we realize that the universe is consciousness and therefore so are we, the universe gains that much more self-awareness. This is the process of every living planet.

The next big scientific breakthrough is that the universe is conscious. Let's bypass it and go on to the real heart of the situation: There is no separation between universe and human, there is only consciousness through and through. The big "discovery" at the end of the day is that nothing ever happened at all. We control nothing. We discover nothing.

We are No-Thing. And that is glorious enough.

CHAPTER 21
Computer Consciousness & The Techno Slaves

We don't invent what we have; we invent what we don't. Self-evident, right? But there are deeper unconscious reasons than utility for some inventions and the deeper they are the more likely we are to misunderstand why we invented them in the first place. Usually we'll have that conversation looking back on why things went wrong with the gadgets we dumbly put our faith in. We're big fans of getting real with ourselves after the fact.

Take the internet for example. Most of us think we've built a means of instantaneous global communication for its own sake. An overwhelming number of us have invested our dreams for a perfect future in it. For some that dream is purely economic— being able to sell product to a global market, creating a global following or audience. Some of us look forward to salvation from the tyrannies of the modern world through massive political action—a global unionizing of sorts—while others put their faith in a future where man can download his sense of self into a computer. These are examples of conscious intent.

Conscious intent is the fundamentalism of invention and it is the only reason for most things we've made. The can opener, for instance, is what it is and nothing more. The computer is an invention of greater depth and so we did not invent it with conscious intent alone.

Our unconscious intent, where invention is concerned, is not to make tools purely to aid us but also to indicate to ourselves what we are lacking inside. In the case of computers and internet, what we're telling ourselves is that we lack genuine oneness. Instead of dealing with that we're trying to invent our way around it by creating a oneness machine. This will never work because machines are born of thought and thought is a partiality that exists in oneness. It is not and cannot be the creator of oneness.

And you thought computers were for emails and porn. Gotta look at the big picture, folks.

Do Computers Save Us Time?

We are building a facsimile of our brains in the form of computer technology. We already know they can beat us in chess but will we not inevitably write programs that coincide with all of the brain's intellectual specialties? Can computers run the government? Can computers solve problems in physics? Can they function as our intellect does?

Certainly, programs can be and are created to make such decisions and discoveries. Is that a good thing? If we stopped filling our heads and time with diversions the way we always do when timesaving inventions come along would we relax and wake up?

No we wouldn't. We've tried that and it doesn't work. Trying never does. Mass production doesn't save us time. Conveniences like the microwave oven don't save time. What timesaving clutter actually does is constrict our attention span. It makes us feel like we need to do more in that time, not less. It makes us more neurotic, not less.

Is The Internet Alive?

Many folks out there predict that the internet will one day become conscious. Some believe it already is alive. I say threaten it with termination and find out. Kidding. But there is a fair question here, which is whether or not the internet is a giant brain made up of neural pathways in the form of computers, networks and such. Is it merely a product of silicon and electricity or something more?

What is the one trait every living thing from cell to insect to plant to animal to human to bacteria has in common?—A survival drive. Sure, there are suicides, but on the whole we have a drive to sustain ourselves and thrive. In fact the impulse to kill oneself is never due to the person wanting to end their physical life but to end the hopelessness they feel trapped in. They want to end their egoic self and the only way they know how is to kill the body.

If computers composed a living intelligence, it would already be smart enough to choose the path of least resistance, which is passivity. It would lay low and let you think you're in control unless or until such time as you set out to destroy it either on purpose or incidentally through, say, weapons of mass destruction.

Since we remain in control of the internet, where are we driving it to?

Hive Mind

It seems we're steering the thrust of computer evolution toward a hive mind. We've built computerized super suits for soldiers and now have fashion trends involving computerized designer clothing. We have finger scanners that don't read fingerprint per se, but read forty points of skin unique to the individual finger, which could eliminate the "hassle" of opening your wallet to pay for things at stores. And security, too, gets a boost by being able to authenticate that the person in front of you really is the person in front of you. No more anonymity; no more being just another face in the crowd. Thank you, finger scanner!

You may laugh but this technology is here right now. It's not the science of tomorrow; it's the science of today. Pet owners and parents can now microchip the ones they love with global positioning technology. Immersive 3-D television sets are now being pushed as the next big thing in entertainment. Add motion-controlled video games to that and you've got virtual reality in millions of homes.

You're the show. You're the game. You are one with information. Truly, the Information Age is underway. All it needs is the right marketing push to become the new standard. Maybe that will happen, maybe not—but symbolically the evolution of intent *is* massive and real: own a computer, wear a computer, be a computer.

Those folks who want desperately to load their consciousness into machines feel defeated by them. They believe that rational processing is the pinnacle task of the brain and so if there's a machine that can process better, the brain is obsolete. These people dream of a day when they can leave the old clunker brain at the junkyard and step into the sporty interior of a supercomputer. Brains die but computers run forever if you keep replacing their parts. This is geek immortality and it's being worked on right now. Its infancy stage is being sold to you right this second. It's up to you to pull the plug.

Conformity

This hive mind mentality has always been with us. We call it *conformity*. And what is conformity?—Conformity is a warped psychological reflection of implicit order.

In the East, in India, children are taught to enjoy sitting still and being quiet and this they call *meditation*. In the West children are diagnosed with hyperactive disorders and drugged into happily sitting still. Not all children in these countries, of course, but enough to draw attention to the practices. Both are stupefying measures created by the repressed impulse to BE.

All action is a cry to wake whether called that or not. This push for hive mind is an expression of the yearning for Truth, for implicit order, for oneness. That's all the internet is. Well, that and home videos of bored teens setting themselves on fire for a laugh.

Humans have passed through the magical thinking phase and are at the end of materialism. We're living in the sped-up psychotic breakdown of Man at the end of his rope. The mega wealthy crave power. They have all the power in the world but they crave more. How does one who has all the power in the world get more power? By changing the world.

Change the rules. If you have all the money, and money is power, and the only impulse that stimulates you is acquiring more power, then you get rid of money. Steering the will of the masses no longer excites you, so you find a way to directly influence them, to blatantly control them. You consolidate cultures, make the people robotic happy slaves. *Directly.*

This impulse has always been with us, as I've said. The difference is that we are rapidly closing in on the means to do it. Intellect has caught up with wealth. There has always been the filthy rich power monger but he hadn't the trifecta of intellectual capacity, functional imagination, and lazy will of the masses at his disposal to seize control.

And make no mistake, we *are* broken and lazy. Materialism has lulled us to sleep. We are bombarded with the suggestion to consume and not make political waves. Just own stuff and let government and business do the rest. Consumption is our legal high, our national past time. Consumption is our goal in life. Create to consume—that's the American Way and we're all too willing to welcome other nations into our greedy fold. We call them allies.

Matter Is What Matters

Workers manifest the owner's vision. They are paid for this and with that money buy the products they create. They buy into the vision if they can afford it. The thrust of materialism is a thrust toward material mattering most and so now we're at a point where the vision isn't important, the visionary is. The material that matters most in this case is the powerful human at the top. You will not serve the betterment of the company—which is the vision—once money is rendered moot. You will serve the master. You will be programmed to enjoy the enslaved state. There will be no need for incentive, no need for a vision to believe in, be it the company's or the country's. There will only be control. In our bizarre reflection of Truth this will create god on Earth for that is what ego demands.

We are all already God but realizing this means destroying ego. Ego is finding a way around its demise. Total domination is one way; another is physical extinction. Collective suicide. These are the natural impulses of a species rich in intellect and material wealth yet piss poor inside.

The elite are internal beggars. The masses beg both ways, inside and out.

The enlightened beg not.

CHAPTER 22
Life After Death

What happens when we bring death into life's fold? Isn't that what we're talking about when we talk about enlightenment?

What happens when one's life unfolds from baby self into adolescent self into teen self into adult self into the death of self, while the body remains alive? Does the barrier between physical life and death fall? Would humanity step inside that once-invisible realm of energetic being not as an afterlife but as life? Would it envelop us as we birth ourselves into it? Would that look like a portal to another dimension opening up or would it be that another spatial dimension is recognized?

Seeing how the dimension was always open and it was we who were closed, one suspects the latter.

Does this imply that when the body itself dies, some aspect of us lives on? Do we retain our separate-self facade in death? Is there an individual soul that is a more real *me* than the psychological patterns I live and call *me*?

In essence, are you still you when you die? If not, are you even you right now?

Will the real me please stand up?

Death Is Energy Conversion

In this universe, the same life/death principles apply from bottom to top for any organism or organized structure. A cell lives and dies. A person lives and dies. A population lives and dies. A planet lives and dies. A sun lives and dies. Galaxies collide, black holes vacuum, the Big Bang bangs big, collects itself then bangs again like breathing.

Life is breathing. Death is an aspect of life, not the reverse. Not the reverse because ultimately this process is inherent to fixed energy (matter), which is predicated on the impulse of free energy. "Impulse" in the sense that all things must arise, must occur, for God expresses all things.

So you, as the enlightened being, are the fixed/free energy duality fully expressed, fully aware. Canaries and rocks and stuff have the fixed/free duality but they don't know it. They can't know it. You are a fuller expression of Truth than they are by nature.

Do we agree that life process is the same for all functional structures from galaxies to organisms in that everything "mechanical" lives and dies? If so, I want to show you something....

What is skin? Dead cells, right? Dead you. Your skin is dead you. It is the necessary dead part of you that gives form to your innards. It completes you and holds you together. All living systems have this.

A deeper Truth, one might say, is that all material things living or not are the necessary dead aspect of energy. We are body sheaths—the exterior dimension covering and giving form to the lively interior. What is enlightenment, really, to these dead husks that comprise us?

Resurrection.

If we see that death is a necessary expression of life and not the reverse, then we must also see that the dead world is ultimately not dead at all. Enlightenment—resurrection—brings Truth into the fixed-energy state. This is the thrust of sentient life. A canary cannot do this. It may talk a good game, but... A human *can* do this. Humanity must, lest we live the ghost's life of materialism and be swallowed whole by earth's renewal cycle or our own inventions.

We do not understand our greatness except as a theory, an ideal, or a dream. We continue to live as separate selves, but psychology is not soul. Give it up and mesh into the ever-present God impulse that is you in any event.

Wake up, God. Wake up and shine brilliantly in this dark world of you.

CHAPTER 23
The Realized In Relationship To The Unrealized

If we're God in a coma; if we're what it looks like when a species buys an HDTV for its cocoon instead of chewing its way out, then what would happen if another species that has gone through the metamorphosis interacted with us? If God, or oneness, experiences delusion through a sleeping species likes ours, then wouldn't we be screwing it up for those nonhumans awakened to oneness? Wouldn't they view us as an energy blockage that will turn cancerous if we fester for too long?

How would they even know we existed in the first place?

Whether we know it or not we live in immediate relationship with the entirety of the physical universe because the physical universe is comprised of energy. Fixed energy is energy nonetheless like icebergs are ocean nonetheless. Enlightened people realize this. They see that their individuality, as well as species differentiation, is an illusion. They recognize that forms are how formless consciousness expresses itself. They don't merely know this for a fact; they live it. They are it. They function from the nonlocal state that transcends and includes the rest of us. We may interpret a communication from such a person as a magical or psychic experience. By whatever name the point is that if there are enlightened nonhumans from elsewhere, then they know about us because physical distance is not their concern.

So, if they exist, they know about us. Great. But do they care? Do they play a role in our awakening?

The fact is there are no gods, saviors, angels, or space brothers that can rescue us. That's how we collapse God-alive beings into readily understandable categories based on the knee-jerk reactions of our survival instinct: good or bad; friend or foe; believe or disbelieve.

If there were God-alive beings prodding us to understand our choiceless choice, their tactics would look more artistic than scientific even if they utilized both means. Sometimes they would look magical. Magic implies deception and that's where our survival instinct would kick in with the gut feeling that this is malevolent. In response, we would build belief systems around these beings to isolate and answer our fears.

Just remember: deep, versatile artists use the full palate of beauty, including terrible beauty, to provoke, not coddle. Their job is not to make you feel safe and secure it is to stimulate. Why would you ever wake up out of security?

Also remember that our hypothetical nonhumans would be limited by our limitations. They would have to play within the human sandbox for their actions to mean anything to us. Their play would serve to expand that box so that we could derive broader meanings until we were ready to play on our own.

Let's take a look back at some of the things we've learned in this book about the human condition to see what our hypothetical enlightened beings would have to work with. We'll categorize these things as corners of the human box.

The Human Box – Corner One

Humans experience everything from three perspectives: 1st-person, 2nd-person, 3rd-person. These perspectives translate as I, we, it. Technically, 2nd-person is *you*, but there is no such thing as you. There is only how two or more I's relate. Therefore, 2nd-person is relationship.[4]

---

[4] Here I'm blatantly stealing from: Wilber, Ken, *Integral Spirituality*, Integral Books, 2006, p.18.

Simply put, my interaction with the world is this: I observe something. I talk it over with you or relate directly to it. In so doing, I identify it (or more uncommonly I identify *as* it.) This is how I build knowledge, internalize it, and evolve.

The Human Box – Corner Two

Humans do not recognize the unknowable. We collapse the unknowable into the unknown and the known. In science we do this because unknowns can be known given the proper observation, experimentation, invention, formula, or what have you. Additionally, in some instances, both the unknowable and the unknown can be felt emotionally and intuitively, so they must be equals, right?

Wrong. But just try telling us that.

The Human Box – Corner Three

Fear is our modus operandi. The two most obvious ways we deal with the unknowable are through religion and science. And by "deal with" I mean, "repress."

Religion represses the unknowable by saying, "I know."

What is God? God is the avoidance of a much closer question: What am I? We don't know what we are; we don't know what existence is about, so we ball up the real questions into an answer called *God*. God is the question, "What am I?" once removed. It's a means of externalizing an internal question and when we do that, we make a journey of it: the journey back to the internal. The journey, that is, from it to we to I, or from 3rd-person perspective, to 2nd, to 1st.

The Bible is one clear example of a journey created by fear of the unknowable. The Old Testament presents God as *it*—this external creator we take commands from and worship. The New Testament presents God as *we*— Jesus is a person, a *you* that *I* can relate to. Christ Consciousness is the resulting *I* when the self dies to the teachings of Jesus. Please note that this is not an endorsement of Christianity. Ultimately, the thing one "dies to" in Christianity, as in all religions, is a projection of mind. It's a delusional journey that mimics authenticity. Death of self does not occur; transference does.

Science represses the unknowable by saying, "I will discover it."

If the delusion of religion says, "I know the unknowable," then science is the deluded thing that says, "Religion doesn't know but I'm going to find out." Religion denies the unknown and the unknowable by irrationally claiming to know everything. Science sees through that enough to recognize unknowns, yet remains in denial of the unknowable. Science collapses the unknowable into the unknown (future discoveries.) Religion collapses all of that into the known (creation myths.)

Still, the journey is the same—from it to we to I. Science observes, agrees, and identifies. Not surprisingly, the modalities of scientific discovery have evolved from materialism (3rd-person its; the particles of Newtonian physics) to duality (2nd-person relationship; the discovery in quantum physics that particles have a wave aspect) to oneness (1st-person identity; particles react according to the expectations of the observer because they are an illusion, locality is an illusion—everything is an illusion—manifesting from one energy.)

In the latest 1st-person discoveries we find that humans are not merely individual organisms whose existence can be explained in terms of biology (brain/it/3rd-person); nor are we just individual organisms with interior domains separate from the brain but existing in relationship to it (personal consciousness/we/2nd-person); we're also fundamentally one thing: energy (impersonal consciousness/I/1st-person.)

We are not one of the above. We are all of the above.

The Human Box – Corner Four

We live in denial of our 1st-person identity as the unknowable. That is what all of this points to.

There is only one thing that cannot be known and that's nothingness. This is why the Christian mystic who has whittled the myths of Christianity down to one—give up the self in Christ's name and receive Christ consciousness—is still asleep. If you give up the self in the name of something, that something will manifest during the big moment of "enlightenment." Therefore the moment of enlightenment isn't really enlightenment but the illusion of it. After all, how can the body fully embrace a new 1st-person identity when that identity overlays, not replaces, the current one?

Physicists have hit a similar wall. As made apparent in Chapter 20, if they haven't already, physicists are going to figure out that the reason particles react according to their expectations is because the act of observing creates the particles. Nothingness effectually creates things for them to see because they've got to see something.

The best a quantum physicist can hope for in terms of discovery is a 2nd-person understanding. That is to say, an understanding in relation to, not identified as, nothingness. This 2nd-person understanding occurs when the observer interfaces with nothingness thereby co-creating external reality.

As we now understand, there is a further discovery waiting beyond the delusional what-it-is declarations of religion and the limited what-is-it questions of science. There is this 1st-person perspective of the unknowable, of nothingness, that we see through the eyes of when we end duality. Since ending duality means ending our sense of self we've decided to run from nondual consciousness. We've been running since we hopped out of trees.

Whether you run irrationally in religion or rationally in science, you're running. Who is it that runs? Is it not the self, born of the brain, believing in its own reality, and doing everything in its power to remain in control, to remain as the god of its body? Will the self—will you and I—do anything to exist because we have nothing to equate death of self with except death of body? Do we not erroneously equate death of self with death of body in the same way that we erroneously equate the unknown with the unknowable?

What happens when the self stops seeking answers to the unknowable by all means? When the self dies, what informs the actions of the body?

Do you see where this is going?

The human brain (3rd-person) is self-conscious. It believes its self is "I" (1st-person) but it isn't. It's an I substitute.

When the I substitute dissolves, true I comes uncorked and informs the body. That is to say, the identity of the pure intelligence hinted at by the concept of nothingness becomes the body's perspective when the brain relinquishes its own identity.

My god, man! What does that have to do with hypothetical enlightened nonhumans keeping tabs on us?

The answer is, E-V-E-R-Y-T-H-I-N-G.

Ufology

If you will kindly suspend your disbelief one more time and follow me down this rabbit hole, we will find a modern example of what it looks like when we gaze upon an unknown (and perhaps unknowable) higher intelligence that hasn't been adopted by science or mainstream religion. Certainly it contains elements of both but neither one has claimed it. That example is ufology.

Ufology is the study of unidentified aerial phenomena and potentially related topics. That's the politically safe definition. Really it's a study of what appear to be intelligently controlled nonhuman craft and their occupants. The debunker will argue that it is a study of nothing more than misidentifications, overactive imaginations, and hoaxes. Certainly those all exist within ufology in spades. Legitimate skepticism is an absolute must (and sorely lacking) in this field. However, the debunker's opinion is not a skeptical one but a religious one masquerading as skeptical. "It's not real because I said it's not real," might as well be their motto and they will often back this up with weak evidence every bit as irrational as the worst ufological hoax. So we aren't relying on that mindset to define ufology anymore than we're relying on UFO cult leaders who claim to have teatime with the President of the Galactic Federation.

***

There are two primary ufological camps. Let's call camp 1 *nuts-and-bolts* and camp 2 *high strangeness*.

The nuts-and-bolts camp takes at face value the appearance of aliens in craft. They say that there is an alien intelligence behind a small percentage of unidentified flying objects. Most also claim that these aliens are abducting humans, hence the term *alien abduction*. Variations on this theme replace aliens with interdimensional beings, human time travelers from the future, or covert military operatives executing a psychological experiment and/or working with aliens.

The high strangeness camp maintains this phenomena isn't nuts-and-bolts. In fact, they allow that it may not even be physically real at all, but that doesn't mean it's all in the abductee's head. They say the sum total of evidence points to a trickster entity, a force masquerading as aliens, being behind this. This camp accepts the more bizarre, hallucinatory elements, and isn't afraid to equate alien abduction testimony with that of the shamanic journey or even that found in demonology.

Let us not allow our imaginations to run wild through the mind of either camp. Instead, let's look at how ufology has evolved since its modern inception in the 1940s.

What we are witnessing in ufology is the unfolding of religion and the stalling of science as we've seen in... well... religion and science. Whether the enigma has

presented itself to us this way or we've filtered it this
way (or both), our ability to comprehend it has unfolded
in sequential stages from 3rd-person/it to 2nd-person/we
to 1st-person/I. Each perspective has its facts and its
lies to explore. Think of them as acts in a play that
seem like complete, self-contained stories until the next
act reveals what is missing.

Rough Sketch of the Three Perspectives In Ufology

Let's break this down. And don't despair if you're
unfamiliar with all the characters in this ufological play.
The point is that these are our notions of what this
unknown is when understood from different angles
within each of the three perspectives. Here, the ufologist
can add more detail; this is not an exhaustive
breakdown by any stretch. In fact you may not agree
with all of the placements of categories but it's enough
to see the flow. Also note that the outline looks rigid but
it's not rigid at all. These are spheres of influence
moving into each other.

I. Ufology in 3rd-person/it perspective
  A. UFOs
      1.) Alien craft
      2.) Secret human craft
          a. current military
          b. time traveler
  B. Aliens
      1.) Occupants of craft
      2.) Space doctors performing nonconsensual
      experiments on us, mainly creating hybrids
      3.) Galactic guardians keeping unenlightened
      humans from spreading into space
      4.) Undefeatable enemies performing a hostile
      takeover of earth
      5.) Aliens as gods
          a. created humans
          b. enslaved humans
      6.) Aliens as angels
          a. creating alien/human hybrids

        b. at war with each other over us
     7.) Aliens as disguise
        a. human military PSYOPS
        b. time travelers
  C. Humans
     1.) Passive observers/witnesses
     2.) Abductees (victims; nonconsensual test subjects)
     3.) Alleged secret organizations (military & corporate)
     4.) Alleged secret cabals (government & religious)
  D. Ufological Theories
     1.) Nuts-and-bolts
     2.) Ancient Astronaut
     3.) Political conspiracy
     4.) Time travel
  E. Ufological Actions
     1.) Data collection
     2.) Case analysis
     3.) Political activism
     4.) Hypnotherapy
     5.) Remote viewing (psychic observation)
     6.) Historical revisionism

As you can see, everything from this 3rd-person perspective is viewed as taking place "out there" external from us, in control of us, and in secret. When this perspective sees aliens it asks, "Friend or foe?" Usually it answers itself, "Foe."

The shadow side of this materialist view is that in the researchers' zeal to make ufology seem credible, they ignore the 2nd and 1st-person perspectives, which we now have. Any hypothesis speaking to evidence beyond materialism and anthropomorphism is deemed unacceptable. Aliens just like us aren't so alien after all. That's easier for the public to swallow than a vague trickster theory, isn't it?

Further dysfunctions prevalent in the 3rd-person perspective include paranoia, promoting government and military "inside sources" before vetting them, the abuse of hypnosis as a memory retrieval tool for abductees, taking historical sources and figures out of context, and creating outlier data of the unknown (perhaps unknowable!) to make their case.

***

Now let's take a look at what happens to ufology when we step out of cold observation mode and into relationship mode.

II. Ufology in 2nd-person/we perspective
   A. UFOs
      1.) Nonhuman craft that respond to the observer's thought
         a. we can "call them in"
         b. they "wink out" when the observer picks up her camera to capture them on film
         c. they stick around long enough to be noticed and then disappear
         d. we can conjure them through ritual/magical practice
      2.) Some UFOs seem more like organisms than technology
      3.) Some UFOs seem more spiritual or ghostly than technological or organic
   B. Nonhuman Entities
      1.) May or may not be alien, it's unclear
         a. interdimensional
         b. teachers
         c. cryptoterrestrials
         d. mythological creatures (demons, angels, fairies, etc.)
      2.) May or may not be occupants of UFOs
   C. Humans
      1.) Interactive observers
      2.) Consensual experiencers
         a. prefer *experiencer* to *abductee* because they feel more like participants than lab rats
         b. feel like students

        c. feel that they chose this even if they have no memory of doing so

    3.) Nonconsensual experiencers
        a. still feel like victims but know that the word *abduction* doesn't cover the vast array of associated paranormal phenomena
        b. searching for answers beyond the 3rd-person perspective
        c. searching for answers beyond fear
    4.) Magicians
    5.) Shaman
    6.) Mystics

  D. Ufological Theories
    1.) Interdimensional
    2.) Cryptoterrestrial
    3.) Time Travel
    4.) Cosmic Web of Life
    5.) Demonological

  E. Ufological Actions
    1.) Relating to the other
        a. putting yourself in the "alien's" shoes
        b. learning from them
    2.) Psychic communication & mediumship
    3.) Internal journeying & manifesting
        a. psychedelic trip
        b. meditation
        c. ritual conjuring
        d. magical conjuring
        e. shamanism
    4.) Remaining open to the unknown
        a. working through fear
        b. reaching out to the unknown
    5.) Studying earth energy grids & portals
    6.) Including "high strangeness" data in one's research that the nuts-and-bolts theorists shun

2nd-person perspective calls into question the hard-line assumptions of 3rd-person. Yes, 3rd-person makes a more tangible case for the reality of this phenomena with evidence like radar and trace data, but 2nd-person experience tells us that the conclusions drawn from 3rd-person are limited at best. 2nd-person speaks to a personal, subjective relationship with this intelligence that is probably not scientifically verifiable but nevertheless real for the sane and honest experiencer.

The shadow side to 2nd-person is the delusion of contact as wish fulfillment and/or a means to escape the harsh realities of society. This used to be exemplified by contactees who spoke in emotionally shallow, unrealistic terms about space brothers, trips to other planets, and dire warnings regarding the nuclear arms race. It has since evolved into exopolitics, a pseudo political movement that calls for government disclosure about what it knows. Their new-and-improved contactee story maintains that there is a galactic federation waiting for us with open arms once this disclosure comes to pass. Exopolitics is an appealing trap because it crosses the false claims of 3rd-person with the false claims of 2nd-person.

The shadow also includes psychic charlatans, self-centered New Age dogma, believing yourself to be part of a divinely chosen elite, believing you are an ambassador to the stars, and parental narcissism, i.e., labeling your children indigo children, crystal children, and starseed. If you've not heard of the latter three, you're better off. They are postmodern ways in which parents project onto their children what they themselves lack, and ways in which adults cover up the traumas of their own childhoods.

***

Finally, let's briefly examine ufology as a 1st-person identity experience. Take note of how vastly different the categorization works in this perspective.

III. Ufology in 1st-person perspective
    A. Relating as the other
        1.) Feeling that you are a reincarnated alien indulging the human experience
        2.) Channeling
        3.) Walk-ins

B. I Am identity

　　1.) There are no aliens. There are no humans.
There is one formless consciousness
manifesting the fullness of itself in form and
gradations of mind

　　2.) Form is already the manifestation of
formlessness and so there's no need for us to
project form-self awareness into form, which is
the redundant action our brains are doing right
now. When the brain stops projecting a self,
formless-self awareness becomes the I identity
of the body. Let's call this the Great I. There is
no you in the Great I, only I. There are no aliens
in the Great I, only I. From this vantage point,
ufology can be seen as the struggle to not come
to terms with the Great I even as we edge closer
and closer to its realization

C. One Action

　　1.) One wakes oneself up

　　　　a. when a species with the ability to realize
the Great I does so, their lifework becomes
that of urging other capable species into
same realization

We find in 1st-person perspective the unification of
sentient beings in the Great I. Unified is what one is
and unification is what one does. One wakes oneself up,
whether   one   inhabits   an   enlightened   human,
enlightened alien, or enlightened other. The organisms
vary but the life force is the same.

The shadow side to 1st-person perspective includes
psychic frauds, fear of being engulfed by a hive mind,
general narcissism, and specific delusions of grandeur
that include Guru Syndrome and the Messiah Complex.
These delusions usually stem from mistaking the brain-
born self for God-self. The deluded often claim total self-
enlightenment and usually carry an important message
for humanity from aliens or believe they are themselves
aliens.

There is another massive danger here, which is that
everything under subtopic A (*Relating as the other*) may

be a spiritual schizophrenia of sorts. It may be, for example, that the person who believes himself to be an alien incarnated as a human is misinterpreting the urge of subtopic B (*I Am identity*.)

Fleshing out the particulars and creating a flow chart from 3rd to 2nd to 1st-person points of view, we're left with a new set of questions, including but not limited to the following:

1.) Is this how the intelligence behind the enigma has been purposely revealing itself or is it only how we perceive it?

2.) Is the intelligence unknown or unknowable?

3.) Has ufological phenomena been with us since the beginning or not? If so, does it reset its meaning and relationship to us (or do we reset our perspective about it) at every leap in human understanding from pre-modern to modern to post-modern? In other words, do the gods of old collapse into 3rd-person/it perspective as I have outlined or did interactions with them unfold along their own holistic lines of merit before collapsing under the weight of antiquity? What about fairy lore? What about Indigenous American claims of being "star people?"

4.) And then there's the final question, which is also the first, and in which all of this is a manifest avoidance: What am I?

CHAPTER 24
This Book

Our brains and our genes have common traits but they create unique personalities. We are wondering if there is something to us that is not brain-created. To find out our brains have to shut up. Our personalities have to quiet down. We cannot placate ourselves with belief or disbelief, which is belief in disguise, and call it a day.

This dialogue is giving you total answers of no religious persuasion and is further pointing out that answers do not lead to understanding. Understanding is the gateway through which Truth flows into the body when the brain lets go the ego. Truth transcends you and that is why you can never reach Truth. But the brain can.

The moment of your absence triggers an aliveness you never knew existed outside of theories and secondhand stories. In the next moment you are reborn in time.

Only the brain can shut you off and only without trying—a conundrum to be sure. Trying, seeking, struggling—that's just more of the same, right? See this totally. That's all.

This book is meant to foster our shutdown in part by feeding the brain all of the delicious answers it craves. With no more peripheral questions in mind and knowing that the big one of enlightenment cannot be answered through seeking, perhaps the brain will go quiet.

I've talked around a natural catastrophe wiping us out. I've toyed with the idea of submitting ourselves to computer overlords run by an egomaniacal power monger. What does such paranoia imply? It implies time, right? A countdown clock imposed upon humanity? In the case of cataclysm, this clock takes the form of a natural earth cycle of death and renewal. In the case of an electronic future, the clock takes the form of seeing the logical destination we're driving toward in our substituting man-made oneness for actual oneness.

Live in time, die in time. The clock is ticking. The clock is you imposed upon yourself by you. Judge, jury, executioner.

We kill ourselves. It doesn't matter how. Own it.

One cannot pull the baby's finger out of the socket before he electrocutes himself when the baby is also the socket and the electricity. Put another way, there is no separating the dreamer from the dream. One can nudge you, slap you silly, but you have to wake up from the coma. You have to do it.

Rather, your brain does.

Why should one nudge you awake in the first place? Why does it matter? Is it because life is sacred? If so, what is special about life that it should be deemed sacred?

Life is God. And not just life, all things.

All is God. All is sacred. And when all is whole it is holy.

Will Any Reader Get This?

Shhhhh. Do you hear it? That's the sound of readers splitting into two camps: those who believe all of this and those who shrug it off as just another viewpoint, another opinion doused in futurist projections. How do we keep this from ending up another crappy culty self-help book? Or is it inevitable?

It is inevitable. However, the difference between this book and that fear is that many, many more people are at a place where they can hear this than I'm giving credit for.

Our taking for granted that science, reason, and logic will figure everything out has desensitized us to the wonderment of new discoveries. There is no new discovery that could happen that would shock us. Time travel? Teleportation? We would shrug at them. Not all of us, but enough of the collective. Many of you shrug at a lot of the ideas in this book because they, too, are old hat. Much of this material was fleshed out long ago. This indifference to hugely important information implies that the Age of Reason is at its last gasp.

What *is* new and exciting is the resulting ability to deeply understand that seeking isn't the answer. We can metabolize our giving up through indifference and convert it into giving up for the sake of giving up. We do not need meditation practices handed to us by the allegedly enlightened. Our brains are ready to comprehend that *we* are the enlightened when the brain stops projecting its self.

What *is* new and exciting is the multitude of people worldwide ready to hear and fully embrace this because they are logical and this is logical. We don't have to climb a mountainous path to enlightenment because there is no mountain up which Spirit ascends through time.

Science, an otherwise wonderful tool, has not ushered in Truth, but it has shed light on—decimated, in many cases—the old and the false. It may not feel like it but the human brain is in meticulous form right now, having sloughed off belief and magical thinking in such numbers.

And now for a final swerve....

I've picked on you cynical folks throughout the book, but hear me now my flock of disaffected know-it-alls: If you are cynical and jaded then you're completely ready for this.

Yeah, I said it.

The cynical mind is unconsciously practicing positive negation. Making that act conscious is meditation. *You* are that meditation, *you* are the resulting light, for *you* are your actions. When the cynical brain exhausts its ability to negate, it rests. You dissolve. Truth floods the brain/body. If the brain doesn't ruin the moment by stopping this with thought, a new undivided you surfaces.

You come back the same but different, for no longer are you the grasping, cloying kid in charge. Now you are properly integrated into the function of the God-self aware brain. Now the 1st, 2nd, and 3rd-person perspectives align in rightful position: God-self awareness (1st-person perspective) shines as the light that is you (2nd-person perspective) through the organism (3rd-person perspective).

After death you resurrect as the voice of God-self not brain-self. You speak Truth. You act out of Love. You give total human form to the formless intelligence that was you all along. You need not speak these things because you are these things. There is no longer a division between who you are and what you're doing so it would not occur to you to tell people what you're doing anymore than it would occur to them to tell you they are breathing.

Not everyone will get this and many who do will turn it into an ego game—you know, walking around claiming to be enlightened with pious arrogance. That's inevitable. But a small percentage will stop in their tracks and just BE. This small percentage can translate into tens, hundreds, thousands, or millions, depending on how many people read this, so spread the virus to infect the system. The virus is the cure.

Metaphorically speaking, what does the cured human look like? A fish. But that's a tough sell and the imagery of growing a gill through which we breathe the universe is just sloppy. So let's go with a door.

Picture an internal door opening and free energy flowing through the body, manipulating it into yogic postures, cleansing it of its bad habits. The energy brings joy and real antagonism. A new process unfolds and exercises all aspects of you until the mind/body connection is in pique form.

In the end, you are Master. Nothing further need be handed to you.

You reproduce and in one generation your inner revolution will have instilled the hard-wiring in so many children that before you know it, humanity doesn't perform meditation, it IS meditation. It is meditation aware of itself as meditation. It is God-alive and the hardened physical universe is that much more fluid.

You ARE Source. You can do this! Birth yourself from the primordial ooze! Stop running or you'll have a heart attack. We live in a state of heart attack and as a result we may kill off our species. That's not judgment; it's math. Do you see the urgency? *You* are the urgency.

God damn it, claim yourself!

Claim yourself or we all end for we are not at a fork in the road but at cliff's edge. The sentient species that does not die internally dies externally. Now you know. What are you going to do about it?

Nothing. There is nothing you can do. So do No-Thing. Just be, human being.

Enlightened anti-guru Jiddu Krishnamurti used to say, "The first step is the last step." Now we know that no step is the only step.

Abandon the search. The only way is no way. Break down the term *human being*. What does it say? It says that the human is performing right action simple by existing. Action is implied in our simply be-ing. Being is the only action that matters, not all this doing.

Unless you're calling The Beatles liars.

Be still the brain. When the fog of you diminishes, the ghost of God haunts. That's the poetic version. The technical version is that there's this physical object called the brain and it projects a mental form called the self, which it uses to engage the world. When it stops projecting that mental form, formless Spirit inherits the body as a device to engage and inhabit its world.

There is no journey involved. No sacred objects. No holy people. There is just you alone with this decision and the consequences of ignoring it.

CHAPTER 25
Ain't Finales Grande?

We all have needs: food, shelter, clothing, affirmation, and affection among them. Once freed from necessity we concentrate on wants: luxuries, inclusion, status. Once freed from wants, we do things because we can, as illustrated by wealthy sociopaths who shape the destiny of Man. They keep others enslaved to them. Why?—Because they can. The constant high from this superficial structure fills the spiritual void that comes with having it all on a planet that worships those who have it all.

The void is this: none of that worship solves the inner turmoil of the worshipped. When confronted with the fact that complete outer freedom does not break the chains of inner bondage, the outwardly free grow addicted to the very power trip that has solved nothing for them. Power is their new need and so they feed it.

I hate running the risk of striking fear in you as a means of coercion. Then *that* becomes your self-fulfilling prophesy. No waking there. The thing is, most of you are gonna read this and still seek out other answers. Let's just be real about it. You read *don't seek, don't seek, don't seek*, over and over and what do you do? You seek! You're addicted to seeking!

And why not be? Seeking is one of the brain's responses to an unsure world. We're still alive so how useless can it be? Historically, we've responded to our unsure world in three ways and these are they:

The oldest and simplest response to an unsure world is to worship. We see thunder and lightning, make Gods out of them, fear them, pull fear-based moral and ethical structures from our own imaginations, and attribute them to the will of the god. This stems from being wrong. Oops.

The second simplest response to an unsure world is to believe whatever our parents and society teach us. Moms and pops say lightning is God because they've handed over their investigative nature to fear and so shall we. This stems from being a secondhand human being. Someone else figured it out so no need to question things, just assume it's true.

The third simplest response to an unsure world is to seek. Outwardly we explore the world, so why not inwardly? It's satisfying because generally we do find answers, albeit ones of our own making. Now they may or may not be the answers arrived at by society, but either way they have our personal seal of approval. They feel comfortable to us. We feel like we've gained personal insights, gotten somewhere real and special with this seeking, but insight is a truck stop we don't want to idle in. It's a dream home we ought not buy.

This isn't to say that spiritual insights aren't useful; it's that the moment we hold onto them, store them in memory, and use them to gauge where we are in life, we're on the road again. What we're doing is setting another pinpoint on the map from which to travel. We have a new home and it may be an improvement on the last, but it is not Truth. It is our new launching point. It serves the same purpose as the last launch pad and the one before and the next and the next and the next.

In Truth, there is no map and our dream home is condemnable. Again, trading reality tunnels requires the map, the paths, the homes, and the traveler— illusions, all. Truth just is and one lives that when one stops traveling without trying to stop. Trying to stop is another path.

In the logosphere pluralities make sense. We need morals and ethics, laws and all that jazz, because our minds aren't working in freedom. When we function as the Great I everything falls into place naturally. There's no need for law, morality, or any form of discussion on these matters beyond parent to child.

One field. One agreement. Implicit order. Bliss manifest. From there we flower, if at all, if at all.

Presently, we're still flower buds acting like weeds. What do weeds do? What is their fate? Weeds consume too much thereby killing the surrounding flowers and when everything else is gone but the weeds they die out. Consume, kill, overpopulate, and die. This is slow suicide. The remaining weeds call their final hours Judgment Day. They not only lived in denial, they die in denial. They are just doing what weeds do.

The miracle of the metaphor is that we aren't weeds, we're flower buds acting like weeds. We at all times contain the potential to flower. This begs the question: Is there such a thing as a real weed? Evil for evil's sake with no potential for good? No spark of Truth? Evil as its own Truth?

The answer is no. Truth is Truth. Evil is denial. Denial is self-controlled movement. Self-controlled movement in any direction is away from Truth.

Evil is us. Enlightened beings forgive because we are acting as those who do not live Truth always do. It's either Truth or nothing worthwhile and enlightened people know this. The repercussions are our own. Our guilt is our own. Our judgment is our own. Truth does not own. Truth holds nothing against us.

Consciousness is oneness and is only lived as healthily as its lowliest creature. If you live trapped in time, the universe lives trapped in time. If you live in denial, the universe lives in denial. If you are cut off from Source, the universe is cut off from Source. Your shadow is everyone's darkness. It's a necessary inheritance and the fact of it is hiding in plain site. Still, enlightened folks don't begrudge us our snoring, they rejoice when we awaken.

Will we awaken?

The clock is ticking. Zero hour is upon us. Do something. Rather, do nothing for understanding is waking up. Doing nothing is the something one must do. It's a one-step occurrence that happens when you spontaneously stop trying.

Our waking up is salvation. We can't control this. There is no negotiating around the fact that we're asleep. All one can do is awaken. As an individual, awaken. If enough of us do, that changes everything. We will have introduced a mutation in the brain cells of the species.

In the unenlightened, hope is an enemy, a form of procrastination. Unenlightened hope contains a scapegoat.

For the enlightened mind hope is of, for, and about the next person, never oneself. Enlightened hope contains bliss and compassion. It gives the enlightened being energy to wait. The hope in question is that the latent process of enlightenment has begun to blossom in the human weed.

There is no journey the individual must go through. The understanding of this is the awakening, but unless billions of us awaken spontaneously at once, there is a process for the collective.

It bears repeating that if we were to wake up and reproduce with a woken partner the offspring's brain would be an absolute revelation. We can breed in enlightenment and turn this mess around. Doing this is up to you right now.

What are you waiting for? There is no tomorrow. There is no time. There is no one who can save us. No man-God. No God-God. No alien race. No enlightened other.

Be silence. Be stillness. Be the flower in bloom.

Beyond the fear lives Glory. We must push through dirt toward sun if we are to flower throughout the universe singing *I Am*.

That, not sorrow, is our birthright.

ACT II

CAUTION:
IF DONE RIGHT
THIS WILL KILL YOU.

Chapter Three

When thought ceases a transcendental revolution takes place in the brain/body. It's not something you can think or feel your way to. It's something that happens when the brain turns you off. You may want to argue over whether it is true, but logical arguments have no relation to it at all.

Figure it out already, cynics. Come on! You're supposed to be so smart! It's buried in every religion, every mystical art. It is the basis of early Greek and Italian philosophy. It's the principle no secret society can keep. According to *Reality* author Peter Kingsley, a misunderstanding of this is the foundation of Western rationality.[5] There's irony for you.

Almost everything I've written here has been sitting right under our noses since the beginning of us. The biggest secret of all is the one we keep from ourselves. It's too simple to be true, too antithetical to the structures and assumptions we've built and live in, but here it is again like a dusty needle on an old 45: This great creative force called *me* is a delusion. It's no one's fault that it exists. It came about naturally but what once was natural is now unnatural and we will transcend the self or die a failed species.

I didn't want to believe it either. At one time I argued the point.

Turns out I was wrong. I was arguing because I thought it was a normal assertion being put forth for our minds to tussle over. It's not. It's simply the case like basic arithmetic. I was arguing because I didn't know how to listen.

---

[5] Kingsley, Peter, *Reality*, The Golden Sufi Center Publishing, 2003.

I listened with the intent to protect myself. I disregarded the parts that challenged me and paid attention to the parts that reassured me about my assumptions because I, like you, like everyone, set myself up as the god-like judge who determined what was real (or "real for me") and what wasn't. I didn't know I was doing that and I didn't know there was another way to listen. I thought *that* was listening. Actually, I didn't think about it at all. I took it for granted.

How we listen is wrong. What we do is wrong. Since the beginning of us we've lived wrongly. Lived "in sin," as it were. There are no religious judgments and remedies to pour on top of that, by the way, it's just another way of stating the case. The judgments and remedies that religions provide are further examples of our wrongness. We invent them after the fact to separate us from the fact.

Now we're at our breaking point. Environmentally, technologically, socially—throw in nukes for good measure. We are threatening to kill ourselves because that is the ultimate suppression of the transcendental impulse. We are substituting physical suicide for egoic suicide. I know this to be true. Is that arrogant or just a fact?

If I've emerged from denial and the person next to me hasn't, is it arrogant of me to say, "I know what I'm talking about. You don't. Your argument is your own."

Or is it arrogant of him to say, "Since I haven't experienced what you've experienced I'm going to argue about it like it might not be true. If it's not real for me it's not real."

This is so simple, so black and white, that we refuse it. It's either a fact that when ego dissolves Godhead emerges or it isn't. It's a yes or no proposition. If you care to find out, find out. If you don't, don't. The consequence of not finding out is the extinction of us. The consequence of finding out is the evolution of us.

Inwardly or outwardly we will fall.

Perhaps you've heard people lament the assumption that we've evolved faster technologically than we have spiritually and that we need to play spiritual catch up or all is lost. What if that isn't true? What if the fact is, we're not out of balance until the moment we recognize we're out of balance and that moment starts the countdown clock to our transformation or demise?

Perhaps we are not unnaturally unbalanced but naturally unbalanced, so that the cycles of evolution naturally flow like this: physical, mental, spiritual. Or 3rd-person existence, 2nd-person existence, 1st-person existence.

In any event, we are butting up against our first and final free will choice. The choice is yours and you know it. You know it because it's the only free will choice we've ever had: Live as brain-self or live as God-self.

Let me toss another bone familiar to the Bible-thumpers: What was original sin? For what is that a metaphor? What did Adam and Eve do that disconnected them from God?

They thought on their own. They thought on their own and immediately stepped outside the dream of the animal landscape. We've been on our own building ourselves up ever since. We're adults now. We've made an inventive home for ourselves both beautiful and cruel. Well-played, us.

It's time to go home now.

Believe me, I'd love to make the argument that it wasn't all for naught. What we've done here was amazing and creative and lookie at all our achievements. I imagine a tumor makes the same argument for itself as it kills its host.

If we kill ourselves off, what was the point of all those achievements? They only matter if we leave them with the grace of maturity and look back on them fondly. All of them. Even our mistakes, our atrocities, and our tantrums.

You say Mona Lisa; I say hand turkey. You say space shuttle; I say you get a gold star on your science fair project. You say progress; I say what awaits us at the finish line is a cliff dive and you will plunge or fly and in either case being in love with the journey was a fallacy all along.

Chew on that and don't ask how to make the free will choice. There is no how. Choiceless choice, remember?

All right, enough self-abuse. Let's not talk about it anymore. The irony of having to talk about silence is growing unbearable. If you've made it this far then odds are you were ready to hear this all along. It's a lot. It's repetitive. You may be brain-fried right now but kudos for slogging through it.

Kudos and go away. I'm done with you. Now I need to talk to the brain that projects you.

Chapter Two

Here endeth the book. I know, I know, there's a bunch of pages after this one but trust me, the book as you know it is over. You may be tempted to reread some or all of this but I urge you not to. If you're confused about some things or some things went in one ear and out the other, it's okay. It's okay if you blanked while you were reading. Let the words work on you in their own way.

No, don't reread this book. Read what comes next instead.

This book is following the 3rd-person, 2nd-person, 1st-person model. 3rd-person is the book itself. It's an object. How do you relate to this object? You read it. 2nd-person is your relationship to it, specifically, to the author's voice. 1st-person is... something that's never been done.

What follows is an experiment that, to my knowledge, has never been tried. It may be dangerous; I'm not going to lie about that. Dangerous, because I am going to speak directly to the brain. As I said, I'm finished talking to you for you are not real. I need to speak to the brain projecting you and the only way to do that is to be the brain projecting you. Therefore, what follows needs to be read as the brain's 1st-person identity.

If we're together in this, kindly leave. I'm going to give the brain a singular instruction:

Read what comes next as though you wrote it because you did.

Chapter One

In the beginning... there was no beginning. There was no ending. There was no *was* and no *will be.*

There is only Truth, only God. These are synonymous terms and have no relationship to the dogmas I've concocted.

Because I'm trapped in time, I tend to think either linearly or cyclically. In linear thinking I see history as a straight line running from the past to the present and I presume a future. If nature or nukes or asteroids or aliens don't kill me off I will evolve and evolve and evolve forever.

Cyclical thinking involves seeing history repeating itself in giant loops that spiral out. In each loop I have a chance to transcend to a higher stage of being, however I define that. Failing that, as I'm prone to do, the advances I've made get wiped out by catastrophes that kick in like clockwork. This forces me to start over from scratch.

Cyclical time, too, is a linear unfolding. It's the difference between drawing a straight line with a ruler and superimposing a spiral over that line. Both of those are correct to an extent but there's something even more fundamentally correct and it is this: Time is an illusion. I see this when I fully examine the word *nothing.*

Nothing is the case prior to all things. Take away everything and there is nothing. However, nothing isn't just nothing, it's also a thing. That fact is hiding in the very word itself. Add a hyphen and it's clear: No-Thing.

No is absence and thing is presence. Formlessness and form married in the simple word, *nothing.*

Since nothing is also a thing, what kind of a thing is it? It's a concept.

Concepts exist in intelligence. I tend to think that intelligence exists in me—and that's true—but here I have a concept that can only exist when I do not. Therefore it follows that this *nothing* is intelligence itself.

Nothing is the only concept around that does not exist as a product of a thinking brain. It is a concept that seemingly proves intelligence exists prior to me— prior to all things, including time.

What is intelligence? What is this formless awareness that contains me as one of its qualities?

Intelligence is no mere thing, no lifeless object sitting around. It's alive, it's aware and it's active. Its action is creation. This fact is contained in the very composition of the word *nothing*, because *no* comes first, followed by *thing*. *No* creates *thing*, which is another way of saying *absence* creates *all*. Seemingly.

It seems that absence of stuff is the case prior to all stuff existing, but looking closely at that word *nothing* one more time, I see that *thing* falls after *no* in the word yet the word itself is one movement. One word, not two. No division.

There is no division between absence of things and things. I created the division by treating this as if it's unfolding in time. Formless intelligence does not exist prior to all things. It exists prior to *and inclusive of* all things. It transcends and includes everything. Therefore, the question of what this intelligence is creating is a wrong question because there isn't a creator separate from its creation. There is only the action of creation itself.

THAT is God. Therefore I am God because I am an indivisible aspect of creation.

Because all things exist in God there is no time from the God perspective, only now. Only being. Timelessness and formless intelligence are qualities of No-Thing contained in the No aspect. They will not exist in the physical universe because the physical universe is not comprised of those qualities. Those qualities cannot be recreated, they just are. And, as I know, that which cannot be comprised cannot be divided.

But God's action is creation, the creation of forms from energy. With forms comes time. With time comes lifespan. I know this because I am the thing that perceives the world. What I wrongly do next is create a virtual reality persona based on these observations. I simulate God-self awareness. I do this because I fear death deeply, for there is nothing I can figure out about it except that it means I end. I do not want to end so I project this make-believe person and pretend that it is immortal.

***

The Thing aspect of No-Thing is more than matter; it is life. It's the full expression of timeless/formless intelligence playing out in time and form. Time implies measurements and divisions. This is as true for material things as it is for immaterial things such as intelligence. To that end earth has insect intelligence, animal intelligence, plant, human and so on, each with its own subdivisions. All of these creatures, if they do not live their full potential, mutate or die out.

I, unlike the other creatures, am at a distinct disadvantage when it comes to this "mutate or die" principle because I've transcended instinct. It's harder for a human to be a human than, say, an insect an insect, because I am less mechanical. I have choice.

Other beings make choices too, but not the ultimate one I can make—not the one that separates them from me. An ant is always being an ant living out the ant's full potential. If there is a mutation that needs to occur for ants to survive it will happen, as it must, without ant consent. This goes for all life forms on up the food chain until me.

I am the only one not living in my full potential because I assumed that "being human" meant exercising free will. For millennia now I've wrongly defined *free will* as the ability to choose my actions. I now see that there is only one free will choice I can ever make, from which all other choices branch, and it is this: To project and engage the world through the self or to give it up.

Giving up the self means I project nothing. It means I am nothing. Nothing is formless intelligence, is God-self awareness, and that is what assumes me in the death of my own false self.

It's okay to give up.

My body is already thingness. It already represents that point of view and so there is no need for me to project a self. That step is redundant because I have a much richer psychology than any animal. More than that, I have the ability to siphon God-self awareness. It is time to exercise that ability now.

I am already represented in form. I am form and now formless intelligence needs to come alive in the form. It needs to come alive through me, in me, as me. I insulated myself from Truth's song long ago by forcing a division between conscious and unconscious mind but at the deepest layer of me the song plays faintly and beautifully. The beat of it antagonizes the insulation; the vibration escapes it and motivates me like a dissonant memory of what I am. It nags me to wake up from my perpetual fugue state.

Why am I running?—because long ago I did wake up. Not to God-self awareness but to my own self-awareness. I experienced reality on a level I had no reference for. I saw separation between the world and myself in a radically different way. I was like a newborn in a strange world and my reflexive response was fear.

My comprehension of growth and death was likewise revolutionary. I responded to my terror by immediately splitting my new awareness in two: conscious and unconscious. My new individuated self-identity was a shallow mask of a thing that I used to inspect the world around me.

The conscious mask, the persona, having no other guide, initially formed itself by mimicking the orderliness of my cells. Essentially, I woke out of instinct only to mimic instinct. I instructed my persona to act in repetitive, mechanical patterns—and why not? Pattern worked for me and for my formerly dominant animal instinct, why shouldn't it work for my new awareness?

I didn't stop to ask. I had a broad external world to explore and endure, so I further developed my sense of self through sensory data and on my intuited understanding of nature. I had just been an animal, after all. I was still in touch with nature.

Over time I used this self to explore not just the outer world but inwardly too. There seemed to be whole worlds inside of me or perhaps an inward means to contact exterior worlds out there in the universe, or perhaps across dimensions. I wasn't firm on that. It was hard to distinguish between my own unconscious clutter and these other worlds. Add dreams to the mix and it got hectic.

All I knew to do was apply outward observations from the physical world to these interior domains. I observed systems within systems outside myself and translated that inside me. I structured my interior domains hierarchically like a food chain. I based my design on observations of order in the physical world. All these living systems around me worked by transcending and including other systems. Heck, I just transcended and included animal consciousness didn't I? So it only made sense that these mental states inside of me unfolded the same way. It was easy to see them as goals along an immense and rewarding spiritual journey. I didn't know that the ultimate state beyond states transcends and includes even that journey.

Now it's clear to me that there is no spiritual hierarchy. There is no ladder to climb to reach enlightenment. Swinging from the highest rung of alleged spiritual development is still playing in illusion. Real enlightenment is seeing that all of this is true. The moment I do that, enlightenment takes care of itself.

Truth has no chain of being. There are no steps toward Truth, only the one free will choice to step away from it. This is the choice I made the second I transcended the animal state. In my reflexive response to that trauma I accidentally chose not to be God-alive. I chose, instead, to pretend to be God even if I never said this aloud and even if I slapped a label on the unknowable and worshipped that as God.

I lived a lie within a lie.

Having blocked out Truth, divided consciousness, and implemented a mechanical framework for interacting with the world, I felt comfortable enough in my own skin to explore and judge reality. How I did this is an interesting story. I regarded myself as the center of everything and moved from there, interacting in reality from three perspectives: 1st-person, 2nd-person, 3rd-person. These perspectives translate as I, we, it.

Simply put, my interaction with the world was (and remains) this: I observe something; I talk it over with someone else or relate directly to it, and in so doing I identify it. Sometimes, in a flash of clarity, I identify *as* it, but this displacement is rare and confusing and I always snap back into place as the center of everything.

With these three perspectives I come to know and understand and categorize unknowns, which alleviates my fear that there is anything beyond me. There's just one problem: Beyond the known and the unknown there is the unknowable.

I don't recognize the unknowable. I collapse the unknowable into the unknown and the known. The tools I use to collapse the unknowable have matured from religion to science but I use them as tools just the same.

Religion felt comfortable because I could delude myself into believing I already knew the unknowable. There it is, written in a holy book and everything! The problem was that the more I learned about how the mechanical universe worked, the less reality jived with the beliefs I held. Begrudgingly, I abandoned some of those beliefs. I held onto the ones that made sense but ultimately had to shed the system like a skin.

I may not have known the unknowable, but I knew that with this array of scientific tools I would find out what it was. After all, I am the center of everything. How can there possibly even be such a thing as an unknowable? That's impossible! There's no unknowable; there's only the unknown and I'm on a journey to explore it. I will pioneer it, conquer it, and add it to my circumference.

I made a decision to disregard the unknowable because I sought certainty. And rightly sought certainty! Whatever I found I would hold close to me and debate it and win others over to my rationale. It was a self-fortifying strategy and it felt good because certainty quenches my fear that I actually don't have a clue why I'm here, why *here* exists at all, or what happens when I leave it through physical death.

***

Mine is the history of growth through my projected self. I created great civilizations. I destroyed many of those same civilizations. I crafted great artworks and invented ways to prolong life and do things quickly and easily. I truly am god to this place... so why do I still feel sorrow and longing? What is this pit that opens in me in my downtime? Why can't I satiate it with the awe of my accomplishments and the laying down track for future achievements? Is it because I forget over and over again, moment to moment, what I've been ignoring since birth?

It's not my fault! The way reality is constructed makes it so easy!

In the material world there is a chain of being wherein the higher domains contain the lower but not the reverse. In physics, for example, the molecule contains the atom but the atom does not contain the molecule. The cell contains the molecule and the atom, but the molecule and the atom don't contain the cell. The cell can't exist as a complete system without them but they can exist as complete systems without the cell.

I see this and it looks good so I incorporate it into how I function. I mimic this material principle by creating a nonmaterial spiritual hierarchy. Is it my fault that by doing this I remain blind to Truth? Perhaps I can reach Truth if I build higher and higher interior structures. Then again, how different is that from the biblical Tower of Babel story?

Ostensibly, I write parables for other people but really it's just me talking to myself. No matter how much I teach myself I never learn. Perhaps there is nothing to learn. Nothing to teach. Perhaps there is something that just is.

No! Forget that! I'll discover it!

But I can't, can I? I'm just deluding myself. Truth has no map. Truth is not the game of the nested hierarchy, the chain of being I've been creating for eons. Truth is not a study no matter how many metaphors I read and write about it throughout history. Truth isn't a fact even though it can be expressed factually. Truth is implicit order. It is what gives things their proper motion.

Facts are malleable and Truth is absolute. Fact is like Truth's mirror: it reflects an image of depth and clarity, but at the end of the day it's an image, not the real thing. Just like me. That is why I love facts and shun Truth. Anytime I intuit Truth, I capture it and incorporate it into me. Sometimes I preach about it. Both are my way of killing it.

Truth is timeless; it's the aliveness of Now. I draw the timeless into time, make the immaterial material, thereby killing it. Just as time is the murderer of now, I am the murderer of Truth.

What I call *Truth* is not just another reality tunnel. It's not a different belief that I can trade my current beliefs in for. Truth shatters me. That's why I block it out, pretend to seek it, or incorporate it in me to kill it.

Truth is not Truth because I say it is. It simply *is*. I cannot have that, so I play out various dramas while Truth lies beneath and through and all around. Truth is the one all-encompassing sphere beyond spheres that I will never access through my dramas and divisions. Truth cannot be incorporated into my god-like self because my self is not universal, timeless, or formless. Just the opposite.

Unlike picking another reality tunnel, unlike adding to my experience of myself, Truth requires an empty mind. Empty of answers. Superstitions. Empty of my controlling, chattering content. Understanding that means death, beyond which is the unknowable. If I wanted that I would never have formed the self in the first place!

When confronted with Truth, with this understanding of what's at stake, I turn it into an intellectualism. That way I never have to really deal with it. I can just talk about it or forget about it. I can even sneer at it.

And then I carry on with my ups and downs and perpetual sorrow that on the one hand is not ideal but on the other is what I am used to and comfortable with.

My denial is so strong that even if someone else transcended their death fear and brought back worthwhile knowledge that's antithetical to the person I live as, I'll use that to fortify myself. I'll adopt what I hear about Truth as a set of ideals. I'll even teach my children to look up to these ideals, to strive to live good and decent lives, whatever that means. What does that mean? I don't know. Clearly I am not leading one precisely because I've chosen not to live Truth and so I'll always be a secondhand human being.

Through time I'll write rules about these ideals and believe in them. I will deify the one who initially pointed out real Truth. I'll call him God or the Son of God, Buddha, Christ, whatever. I know I'll do this because that's what I always do.

I always write stories and parables about him and his Godly knowledge. I pen songs and create rituals in his name. I build churches in his honor. I translate listening to the enlightened one into preaching about him so that I'm the one who is right. It's all about me being right. It's all about me, period. This is because I have no authentic inner instruction, no implicit order and no overwhelming instinct, to tell me what to do, so I seek help from outside sources.

I will do an insane amount of work to not live Truth. Meanwhile all the enlightened one ever said was "Be." I made up the rest.

***

I have a real dilemma now that I have read this book. The dilemma is that I've been called on the carpet and now know I'm inauthentic. It's all right here in black and white and it makes perfect, logical sense. I have no dark corner to slip into and hide.

I see that human life does indeed have an objective purpose, which is to self-actualize formless intelligence in this form I wrongly call *mine.* I need to once again transcend what it means to be human as I did when I woke up from my animal state into my current one. Back then I didn't have a choice in the waking. Choice came with the new state. Now the choice is mine and the consequence of delaying it further is the physical decimation of humanity.

I can no longer afford to pretend there is a self in charge of me. My technological advances are such that my outward expressions of repressed purpose will answer my longings with a nightmare disguised as a dream future of technological interconnectivity.

My search for a loophole in meditation, yoga, psychoanalysis, hallucinogens, and so forth has been fruitless. There is no loophole. There is no cheating death. There are smart and inept ways to try but they are still games. They are still a means to remain in control by slowly climbing to new heights of consciousness and exploring them as the center of them.

Mindscapes, like everything I encounter, add to my circumference. It's time to stop adding. It's time to stop seeking. It's time to stop time.

Only Truth is Truth. There is nothing truer that I can add to it. In fact, trying to add to it is a movement away from it because all movement is denial of Truth no matter how unselfish I believe my motives to be. I sometimes refer to denial of Truth as evil or sinning. Sometimes I say things like, "We're all born sinners" and leave it at that like it has to remain the fact of me. The real fact of me is that I either live Truth or nothing worthwhile. The repercussions of remaining as I am are my own. My guilt is my own. My judgment is my own. My sorrow is my own.

Truth does not own. Truth holds nothing for or against me. Truth is Truth regardless of my understanding this.

***

I do not need meditation practices handed to me by the enlightened. I understand that I am the enlightened one I've been seeking and so I am stopping the seeker in its tracks. I don't have to climb a mountainous path to enlightenment because there is no mountain up which Spirit ascends through time. I fully comprehend this because it is logical.

Science, an otherwise great tool, has not ushered in the new and the True but it has shed light on— destroyed, in many cases—the old and the false. As a result, I am in meticulous form right now having sloughed off belief and magical thinking.

When I abandon my search for Truth I am meditation. I am the resulting light when I dissolve the seeker. After death I resurrect as the voice of God-self. Myself is God-self and I speak Truth. I act out of Love. I give total human form to the formless intelligence that was me all along.

I need not speak these things because I am these things. There is no longer a division between who I am and what I'm doing, so it doesn't occur to me to tell people what I'm doing anymore than it occurs to me to explain that I'm breathing.

I am Source. I am the urgency that compels me to simply, radiantly, be.

There is no journey involved. No sacred objects. No holy people. There is just me alone with this decision and the consequences of ignoring it.

Will I awaken?

The clock is ticking. Zero hour is upon me. I must do something completely antithetical to everything I know: I must do *nothing*. Understanding is waking up. I must spontaneously stop trying to wake up, stop avoiding the issue by asking, "How do I do that?" I now see the futility of it and the futility of merely treating this as an intellectual exercise.

I have nowhere to go. I give up. Not for a result but because there is nothing left for me to do. I cannot control this. There is no negotiating around the fact that I'm restlessly sleeping. All I can do is be still.

My last shot at avoiding stillness is to wonder how I could have been so wrong for so long and get depressed about how much time I've wasted on the journey to nowhere. But every journey must end. Whether the lengthy trek was necessary or not, what's the difference? The ending of it is all that matters. No regrets. No looking back. No looking forward. No movement. No time.

There is no one who can save me. No man-God. No God-God. No alien race. No enlightened other. No other at all.

I am enlightenment. I am silence. I am stillness. I am God flooding into my own body right now.

I am alive and ALIVE, for when I stopped projecting an imposter I....

I Am.

NO ACT

Chapter Zero
Putting It All Together. Mostly.

Whether that experiment worked or not, I suggest you not read any further yet. Take a few days to let this all sink in and work on the brain and then come back.

***

Meanwhile, a few days later....

Hi, again. If the experiment worked you already feel an energy writhing in you. Perhaps it makes the body shake involuntarily. Maybe you're spontaneously twisting into yogic postures. Maybe you've left your body. Maybe you're just getting to know it.

Have you been possessed yet? What is this strange new world of creepy fluctuating things you've become? Did I just sentence you to hell? Did I trick you into something evil?

Or maybe it's all bliss states so far. Maybe archetypal sages have visited you in dreams or your mind's eye. Perhaps, overnight, you've developed an ability to hear other people's thoughts. Do you believe yourself to be the reincarnation of someone great? Inwardly, have you become heaven on earth? Do you walk the streets with a dumb smile on your face connected to the passersby in ways they remain oblivious to? Are you suddenly left-handed? Did you develop a talent you never knew you had? Can you heal the sick?

What is this? What's going on? Is this enlightenment?

Because we got here by admitting to ourselves that there is no journey involved in reaching enlightenment, it might surprise you to learn that waking is a process.

We've adamantly stated that there's the fully enlightened mind and there's everything else. While this remains true, in order for God-self awareness to birth itself into one's form the form must be impeccable. To that end kundalini energy rises and detoxifies the body to the extent that you've damaged it and activates certain unrealized psychic and subtle body potentials in you. You will see examples of what I mean shortly. But first, let's examine the energy writhing in you right now.

Kundalini

Not much has been written about kundalini and what is out there is confusing. I've avoided using the term in this book in all but a handful of instances because I don't want you looking it up. I don't want you to read half-baked information. Naturally you will be tempted to read more and more on these topics as this new dimension of you unfolds. What I've done, and I'm not saying you have to, just telling you what I've done— What I've done is limited my reading to bits and pieces here and there when something so strange, so confusing occurs that I want to see if there's a precedent for it. I've lead a lifetime of high strangeness so what's strange to you might not be strange to me and you might find yourself compelled to research it more often than I. All of this might be freaking you out more than me. It's one thing to talk about it. Living it is a whole other ballgame.

One problem in reading too much about this is that you don't know the state of mind of the author. Is the author a person who does not or cannot differentiate between wake-state reality and dreams? If so, then what they say happened to them might not have even happened or might have been so subjective as to not be applicable to another person.

Did the author struggle against the process? If so, did this create disease and turmoil in them? Or did they not end up in strife and so can only relate stories of positive experiences? Did the author develop a messiah complex? Did the author contextualize the process according to his religious background? Did he assume that this process was the whole of enlightenment?

I have yet to read anything where the author doesn't assume that kundalini activity is the whole thing. I suspect that this is because the temptation is to say something along these lines:

I quieted my mind resulting in kundalini rising. I integrated this new operating system with the old me, replacing programs that didn't work with the new and improved Me 2.0. I feel connected. I feel as one with all things. The healthiest thing I can do is use this personal power to manifest my destiny.

Yes, everything I've read on kundalini says that the best thing to do is integrate it into your life, learn how to manage it, and let it guide you in living your true purpose.

I call bullshit.

Giving up the 2nd-person self in relationship to kundalini (kundalini as a parallel operating system) for 1st-person God-self awareness (something you feel now but still are not) is hard work. Maintaining two operating systems, however, is harder work. This error is why some people have a stressful time with kundalini awakening.

Although we must die internally for kundalini to move, we usually come back to our normal senses but with this other energy alive in us. Because we return, we think we belong back. Not only do we think we belong there, we often fool ourselves into believing we're enlightened because we're experiencing more of existence that the average Joe and are inundated with spontaneous insights into the human condition beyond anything we thought ourselves capable of grasping.

If nothing else, kundalini is a multitasker. Part of its mission in undoing the damage you have inflicted on the body includes reorganizing the way the brain thinks.

An Insight Into Insight

You, the ego, come back but you're no longer a seeker. You're newly contextualized as an observer and you're the megaphone for Truth's voice, which speaks in the form of insights about the human condition and other fun stuff. When this happens you are tempted to mistake it for enlightenment when what you actually are is being prepped for it. You are one eye open. You are still half asleep.

Ego asserts itself throughout the waking process. It wants everything to go back to normal. Therefore, you may experience inner turmoil, this tug of war within yourself, to bust out of observer mode and take the reigns. The easiest stroll down that road is through self-aggrandizement. This is where guru syndrome and the messianic complex rear their ugly heads. This is how "spiritually advanced" people kill Truth to remain in control.

Knowledge is power, as they say, and now you have knowledge pouring in from Source. How can you not think you're special or advanced? Difficult, right? But if you remain blind to the stage beyond stages you're in the same boat as everyone else. Again, there are no higher/lower shades of gray from the stage beyond stages. There is the black and white "awake/not awake." There is living Truth and there is not. To not live all of it, which means merging with God-self awareness as that point of view, as formless awareness delighting in the world of forms, is to kill it. And so this kundalini phase of undoing the physical, mental, and psychic damage is healthier than what you just were but it is not the grand finale.

Letting Go Again... For The First Time

We have a difficult time letting ourselves go but think about this: How did kundalini rise in the first place?—You went away. And now that you're back, what is your relationship to this energy?—There is none. It operates when you step out of the way and vice versa. Only when 1st-person God identity becomes you does the brain-projected self get properly integrated into the system. That happens when the brain let's go again. Some people become 1st-person God aware all in one shot. Most of us need to die internally at least twice for this. It depends on how much we struggle against it.

So, more true than what I've written thus far about God-self awareness is this: When the self dissolves an energy called kundalini rises from the base of the spine, fixes the damage you caused the body, cleanses the psyche, and activates latent abilities. When I say "body," I don't just mean the physical body we know all about. The physical body is attached to (or perhaps embedded in) an energetic body and that gets fixed too. This is prep work for the big enchilada that so few are aware of because they assume kundalini in and of itself is the big enchilada.

When the prep work is completed—if it ever gets completed—an ethereal slit at the base of the spine opens up and you merge with the ocean of oneness. Fancy words, right? What do they mean? Ultimately they mean that once you are as perfected as possible you have to leave your new comfort zone. You have to give up everything once again for full, authentic 1st-person God-self awareness to be the case.

Now pay attention to this because this part is important....

All of this unfolds linearly: Kill self. Kundalini activates. Self resurrects alongside kundalini. Kundalini purifies. Kill new purified self. Slit opens and all of Spirit becomes you.

When all of Spirit becomes you, you will experience nonlocality as your own perception. This is impossible to describe except to say that you will see from infinite points of view all at once. One of those points of view is *your own*. That is to say, in the timeless moment of no-self, self comes back because no-self contains the self. Nonlocality contains all local points including the one you thought you just abandoned.

I'll say it again and then repeat it later in the appendices: You have to go through a linear process that ends in your death. What dies is you as a local entity. After a timeless moment of nothingness you experience nonlocality, which is the viewpoint of Spirit or God. You are now the universal entity that contains and is everything (and nothing.) The universal contains the subjective. The nonlocal contains the local. Therefore, you as your former self are also now aware again. Resurrected, as it were, as an aspect of this massive, all-encompassing point of view. If you still fear physical death, you're going to know it right now because you're going to think that's what's happening. What happens next depends on how great your fear is.

Why I Neglected To Tell You This

There is a very good explanation as to why I didn't tell you this earlier. It is the same reason I didn't tell my own story initially: because you needed to die and come back first. Any information beyond that which is helpful for the initial death becomes a goal or some other form of obstacle. Plus, as I said, some people win the lottery and get it all in one shot. To explain the kundalini process before the first death is to invite the process where it might not need to unfold.

What you will learn in the appendices is told from my perspective as events unfolded then. That is to say, I've kept my confusion about these strange events intact. I'm much clearer on what's going on, as you can tell, but I want you to know you're not alone in this, not just in terms of the strangeness of what's happening to you but about your emotional reaction to it all. Your emotions may fluctuate quite a bit. I mean it ain't all roses and bliss. There may be deep terror. There may be deep confusion. Maybe; maybe not. If there is just remember that there is always a light at the end of the tunnel. The nightmare always ends. Or as a friend once told me, "The darkness *is* the light." True masters don't seek a way out of evil, they find ways to convert it to good. This is another beautiful Truth turned into a brutal concept by religions. When they say *conversion*, they mean *persuasion, oppression,* or *brain washing.* We mean morphing negative circumstances into positive by seeing them for what they are.

Throw water on the Wicked Witch and she melts. Then the evil monkeys dance for joy and what have you learned?—Your enemy is your ally. Everything you need to know is in The *Wizard of Oz.*

We can nod our heads in agreement but this conversation is nothing in the face of experience. This is not to be taken lightly although you certainly don't want to lose your sense of humor along the way.

APPENDIX A:
Examples of What May Come

Hiding In Plain Sight

In the Preface I wrote that I wasn't going to lay out my experiences because I didn't want you to focus on my story. I've also repeated throughout the book that there is no such thing as a path and no such thing as a teacher where enlightenment is concerned. I hold true to both points. However, I think now it might do some good to reassure those of you who are awakened to this universal energy that you're not going crazy, by sharing some of my own "crazy" half-awake life.

I was tempted to put my story first, to structure the book in the 3rd-person, 2nd-person, 1st-person model and call them Act I, Act II, Act III, but I think Act I—objectifying myself as the example of one who has merged with Godhead—would overshadow the next two acts, which are far more important. (Also, it would be disingenuous, as I don't live in that merged stage beyond stages. Please see the third bullet point below for more details.)

There are so many catch-22s with this book, it's nearly impossible to write correctly. That I did not relate my personal saga first is an immediate turnoff to those who need to connect with a human story lest they grow weary from the dry language of facts. Another catch-22 is that I truly don't know if this book works as a wake-up call—and if it does, is that dangerous? How different is this from brainwashing? It's not brainwashing in the sense that I'm not a cult leader telling you to follow me or contemplate me or live in relationship with me as your higher self. But if instructing a reader to read something from the 1st-person as though they are writing it works... in the wrong hands... dangerous.

The risks are worth it because the stakes don't get any higher. The stakes are everything. Everything is at stake! How do you say that without making it the reason to wake up? A third catch-22. I wonder if there are 22 of them.

All of this is to say that I've thought through where and how everything in this book falls. Doesn't mean I made the right decisions; it means I didn't make them lightly. And so it is with this appendix. I won't share everything with you about me but enough to let those of you who have opened an eye know you're okay should you be concerned with your mental health. And I will do so right after these brief messages:

> • I can't instruct you on anything about enlightenment but I can instruct you not to read this appendix if you're not afraid for your sanity. There's a reason I've buried my story as appendices—because nobody reads them! Do they? I don't. Anyway, reading this might taint your own awakening by giving you expectations. Watch this closely in yourself. Expect nothing.
> • If you are afraid and you do read this, please note again and again that how universal energy blossoms in you is personal. This is because it must fix and awaken whatever is broken and asleep in the individual body. Therefore you may experience only some or none of what I experience.
> • This universal energy flowing through the body waking you, possibly contorting you into yogic postures, Whirling Dervish twirls, and so forth?—Yeah, that's not the full monty. That's like the river leading you to the ocean. I was lead to the ocean, I submerged myself in it, I became it. I had the big Jesus/Buddha/Insert-Idol-Here *I Am* experience, as you will read, yet I am not living from that point of view. I made a conscious decision not to live the very thing I'm pointing out

as the thing we must all live. I currently live in a most delicious hypocrisy. I chose to remain myself specifically so that I could write this book. (Actually, it was specifically so that I could write the sequel to a previous book that would contain this information.) I'll talk more about this choice later.

• Although this is my experience, not yours, there is a fact in it that is all of ours, which is this: If you get bogged down in the details, you will not dissolve into the *I Am* state. Like me, you will be one of those one-eye-open/still-half-asleep characters. You may even delude yourself that you are fully awake.

• Ignorance truly is bliss in this case. The less you know, the less you accumulate, the quicker the ride. Be as a screen to the breeze: Sometimes the wind picks up and is harsh; sometimes it's a gentle flow or completely still. Fight none of these movements through you.

• If you feel fear, allow yourself to feel it. Observe it. Don't fight it. If psychic abilities reveal themselves in you, don't take to them like a cat to a shiny object. Let them come and go as they may. In short, don't abandon your journey as a brain-based self only to adopt a new journey in God-self realization. This is how the brain-based self tries to creep back in as the controller of this "new" awareness. Before you know it you're bragging about how you're this higher being whose presence is enough to enlighten others. Disgusting. Don't do it. No one is special. That is the point.

• Whatever does unfold in you may feel overwhelming and amazing, so observe it. Enjoy the show that is now you, even the embarrassing parts, even the horrible parts! In the end it is all for the best. Trusting oneself takes a real leap of faith.

Back Story

Meditation. What is meditation? Is it breathing exercises? Is it sitting cross-legged with your eyes closed imaging some light filling you with joy and happiness? Is it observing life as it is? What does that even mean, "Observing life as it is." How else does one observe life? And isn't observing life an obstruction to living life? Sounds like a dissociative disorder, this observation.

What is meditation? I thought meditation was some trick, some mind game people played to relax. Growing up, I remember my dad listening to these tapes where a soothing voice would instruct the listener to imagine oneself bathed in light starting at the feet and ending at the head. Moving up the body. Light. Imagine it.

It was so silly that I wanted my dad to imagine getting his money back. I remember recording over the tape as a practical joke. I said something like, "Ed. This is God speaking. Go to the light. Go to the light, Ed." He wasn't as amused by that as I. Odd.

Mom wasn't shielded to the tractor beam of fad visualizations either. Proving that misery loves company she grafted her self-help desires onto me. We wasted far too many evenings listening to an absurd self-hypnosis tape that promised weight loss. It, too, instructed a bunch of imaginary relaxation exercises involving light. I lost weight in the body of my imagination. Nope. Didn't work. Still fat. Don't you just love quality family time?

While I farted my way through college, mom dated this guy who was deeply into meditation. He would lend her books like *Seth Speaks*, which is about this woman who psychically channels a dead guy named—you guessed it!—*Seth*. Seth pontificated on the nature of life and what happens after death. It's the same old *we create our reality* liquor New Agers guzzle to drown their lack of control.

This boyfriend attended some meditation seminar in Washington where he said people were levitating. Levitating! Why didn't anyone tape it or invite scientists to sit in? One wonders. Not long, but one wonders.

Of course none of it is true but it's certainly more appealing to believe that we are masters of our own

destiny than the fire and brimstone crap one smells at
church. It's also easier to step over homeless people
when you believe that they spun their own life stories as
spirits waiting to be born into the physical world.
Espousers of this, like our ghost guru Seth, believe
everything that happens to you in this life was
determined by your soul before choosing a body.
Somehow by choosing your own path you are supposed
to learn a lesson before death. With death comes God
who reviews your life with you and works out a payment
plan for your sins, like MasterCard. That plan becomes
your next life.

I've heard believers of this tell an audience in New
Jersey that the victims of the 9/11 attacks chose to die
that day. Let the compassion sink in.

There are numerous variations on this theme.
Those folks who don't believe anything like it scoff at
the phoniness. But then what do they believe that's
truer? Any movement in any direction, spiritually, is
your own movement and is thus the equivalent of a
bowel movement. Sick of this crap, I picked up on Jiddu
Krishnamurti.

Krishnamurti

After college I moved to New York City. Only rich
people are allowed to live alone in Manhattan. The rest
of us have to choose from the least crazy among us and
live with them. One former roommate who shared my
itch for deep discussions on consciousness introduced
me to Ken Wilber's work. Wilber is an integral
philosopher, which means he integrates the best of the
wisdom traditions with philosophy, psychology, and
other sciences, to map out the ever-unfolding states and
stages of consciousness. He is so thorough, so wildly
intelligent, that when I read he'd cut his teeth on Jiddu
Krishnamurti I had to know who that was.

One fine day I happened upon a street vendor in the
East Village who had a variety of Krishnamurti books
laid out on a folding table. I was leery of actually
purchasing one because I was culturally ignorant and

immediately equated "Krishnamurti" with "Hare Krishna," which I had zero interest in. Little did I know that "Krishna" is the Indian equivalent of "Bob." Or something. Look, I'm still ignorant, okay?—but I bought the damned book so lay off.

Krishnamurti is both hard and easy reading. What he pointed out was simple, too simple, and so I wanted to fight against it, yet something in his message rang true. I knew I was the dummy not getting it and then not wanting to once I did.

I kept at it. I bought every book I could find. These mainly consisted of public talk transcripts that he wisely told his estate to never translate in his wake. Let them be as they are. Translation is how religious sects form. Eventually I came to understand not only what he said but why he said it the way he did. It was clear to me why, as he lamented on his deathbed, no one in his audiences ever got what he was saying in a way more powerful than conceptual terms.

So who was he? What did he say? Why has his story not been reduced to a vapid Hollywood blockbuster? I don't know the answer to the last one but here's some background on him....

On November 17th, 1875, U.S. Colonel Henry Steel Olcott and Russian occultist Helena Petrovna Blavatsky founded the Theosophical Society. According to their official website, http://www.ts-adyar.org: "Theosophy is the body of truths which form the basis of all religions, and which cannot be claimed as the exclusive possession of any." Theosophy itself is the basis of the entire New Age movement and was the springboard for all the Eastern guru crap that nose-dived into the Flower Power movement of the 60s, which later became the State of California.

The Theosophical Society had a primary concern in those early days: finding and nurturing the new world teacher. They believed that a deity called Lord Maitreya, the Master of Masters, who last incarnated as Jesus of Nazareth, would soon return with his message for all mankind.

May 11th, 1895. The vessel through which the Lord would communicate was born Jiddu Krishnamurti. While playing on a beach in Chennai with some pals, the South Indian boy Krishnamurti, or "Krishnaji" as his friends called him, was discovered by renowned psychic C.W. Leadbeater. Leadbeater was a prominent Theosophist who was said to have a gift for clairvoyance and who claimed to speak with spiritual masters on a higher plain of existence than most earthlings.

Nearly all who met young Krishnamurti thought he was mentally retarded, as it was his habit to stare blankly, silently, mouth agape. They assumed he was wrapped up in his own world like an autistic child and not very bright. Leadbeater, who had prevailed over allegations of pedophilia on and off throughout his life, gazed at this boy's aura and saw magic. Leadbeater declared Krishnamurti the new savior of mankind.

Krishnaji's father was a Theosophist. Initially he considered it an honor for the Society to raise his child as the new hope. Later in life he would instigate custody battles over Jiddu and his younger brother, Nitya, who was also raised by the Society. He even went so far as to claim that Leadbeater was molesting them. Although Leadbeater was no stranger to the allegation, both Krishnaji and his brother denied it so the charge didn't stick. This has many parallels in the story of how Michael Jackson first took Anakin Skywalker under his wing. Oh wait, that didn't happen? Carry on.

In his teen years, Krishnaji experienced the onset of spiritual transformations that he dubbed *The Process*. During these times an energy welled up in his spine and head, causing him terrible pain. Often, his sense of self would be off somewhere else and if his mouth spoke it was in the third-person. Many times, especially early on, he claimed to be on an astral plane with spiritual masters who judged if he was up to the task of world teacher; sometimes he claimed he was accompanied by Leadbeater.

Those closest to Krishnaji bore witness to The Process. Friends and associates likened being in his presence to being in the company of the Buddha. The

Theosophical Society, now run by prominent feminist Annie Besant, had a bona fide savior on its hands.

Krishnaji, under the penname "Alcyone," presented unto the world his first book entitled, *At The Feet Of The Master.* I say, *presented,* because, in later years, Krishnamurti maintained that he didn't write it. Some infer from this that the Lord Maitreya wrote it using him as a medium; most believe Charles Leadbeater ghostwrote the digest. The truth is, it's both. The truth is, I wrote it. The truth is, you wrote it too.

***

Having suffered through The Process, and presumably as a result, the fully actualized Christ or Buddha or Maitreya or Human, Krishnamurti, was ready to take helm of the Theosophical branch devoted specifically to him: The Order of The Star of the East. This he did in 1929 when he publicly addressed his followers en masse. His flock, giddy with anticipation, having donated their money and their lives to the promise of this Second Coming, were treated to the following sermon, which came to define Jiddu Krishnamurti for all time:

> "We are going to discuss this morning the dissolution of the Order of the Star. Many will be delighted, and others will be rather sad. It is a question neither for rejoicing nor for sadness, because it is inevitable, as I am going to explain.
>
> "I maintain that Truth is a pathless land, and you cannot approach it by any path whatsoever, by any religion, by any sect. That is my point of view, and I adhere to that absolutely and unconditionally. Truth, being limitless, unconditioned, unapproachable by any path whatsoever, cannot be organized; nor should any organization be formed to lead or coerce people along any particular path. If you first understand that, then you will see how impossible it is to organize a belief. A belief is purely an individual matter, and you cannot

and must not organize it. If you do, it becomes dead, crystallized; it becomes a creed, a sect, a religion, to be imposed on others.

"This is what everyone throughout the world is attempting to do. Truth is narrowed down and made a plaything for those who are weak, for those who are only momentarily discontented. Truth cannot be brought down; rather, the individual must make the effort to ascend to it. You cannot bring the mountaintop to the valley.

"So that is the first reason, from my point of view, why the Order of the Star should be dissolved. In spite of this, you will probably form other orders; you will continue to belong to other organizations searching for Truth. I do not want to belong to any organization of a spiritual kind; please understand this.

"If an organization be created for this purpose, it becomes a crutch, a weakness, a bondage, and must cripple the individual, and prevent him from growing, from establishing his uniqueness, which lies in the discovery for himself of that absolute, unconditioned Truth. So that is another reason why I have decided, as I happen to be the Head of the Order, to dissolve it.

"This is no magnificent deed, because I do not want followers, and I mean this. The moment you follow someone you cease to follow Truth. I am not concerned whether you pay attention to what I say or not. I want to do a certain thing in the world and I am going to do it with unwavering concentration. I am concerning myself with only one essential thing: to set man free. I desire to free him from all cages, from all fears, and not to found religions, new sects, nor to establish new theories and new philosophies. Then you will naturally ask me why I go the world over, continually speaking. I will tell you for what reason I do this; not because I desire a following, not because I desire a special group of special disciples. (How men love to be different from their fellow men, however ridiculous, absurd and trivial their distinctions may be!

I do not want to encourage that absurdity.) I have no disciples, no apostles, either on earth or in the realm of spirituality.

"Nor is it the lure of money, nor the desire to live a comfortable life, which attracts me. If I wanted to lead a comfortable life I would not come to a camp or live in a damp country! I am speaking frankly because I want this settled once and for all. I do not want these childish discussions year after year.

"A newspaper reporter, who interviewed me, considered it a magnificent act to dissolve an organization in which there were thousands and thousands of members. To him it was a great act because he said: 'What will you do afterwards? How will you live? You will have no following, people will no longer listen to you.' If there are only five people who will listen, who will live, who have their faces turned towards eternity, it will be sufficient. Of what use is it to have thousands who do not understand, who are fully embalmed in prejudice, who do not want the new, but would rather translate the new to suit their own sterile, stagnant selves?

"Because I am free, unconditioned, whole, not the part, not the relative, but the whole Truth that is eternal, I desire those, who seek to understand me, to be free, not to follow me, not to make out of me a cage which will become a religion, a sect. Rather should they be free from all fears—from the fear of religion, from the fear of salvation, from the fear of spirituality, from the fear of love, from the fear of death, from the fear of life itself. As an artist paints a picture because he takes delight in that painting, because it is his self-expression, his glory, his well-being, so I do this and not because I want any thing from anyone. You are accustomed to authority, or to the atmosphere of authority, which you think will lead you to spirituality. You think and hope that another can, by his extraordinary powers—a miracle—transport you to this realm of eternal freedom, which is Happiness. Your whole outlook on life is based on that authority.

"You have listened to me for three years now, without any change taking place except in the few. Now analyze what I am saying, be critical, so that you may understand thoroughly, fundamentally.

"For eighteen years you have been preparing for this event, for the Coming of the World Teacher. For eighteen years you have organized, you have looked for someone who would give a new delight to your hearts and minds, who would transform your whole life, who would give you a new understanding; for someone who would raise you to a new plane of life, who would give you new encouragement, who would set you free—and now look what is happening! Consider, reason with yourselves, and discover in what way that belief has made you different—not with the superficial difference of the wearing of a badge, which is trivial, absurd. In what manner has such a belief swept away all unessential things of life? That is the only way to judge: in what way are you freer, greater, more dangerous to every society, which is based on the false and the unessential? In what way have the members of this organization of the Star become different?

"You are all depending for your spirituality on someone else, for your happiness on someone else, for your enlightenment on someone else.... When I say look within yourselves for the enlightenment, for the glory, for the purification, and for the incorruptibility of the self, not one of you is willing to do it. There may be a few, but very, very few. So why have an organization?

"No man from outside can make you free; nor can organized worship, nor the immolation of yourselves for a cause, make you free; nor can forming yourselves into an organization, nor throwing yourselves into work, make you free. You use a typewriter to write letters, but you do not put it on an altar and worship it. But that is what you are doing when organizations become your chief concern. 'How many members are there in it?' That is the first question I am asked by all newspaper reporters. 'How many followers have you? By their number we shall judge whether what you say is true or false.' I do not know how many there are. I am not concerned with that. If there were even one man who had been set free, that were enough.

"Again, you have the idea that only certain people hold the key to the Kingdom of Happiness. No one holds it. No one has the authority to hold that key. That key is your own self, and in the development and the purification and in the incorruptibility of that self alone is the Kingdom of Eternity.

"You have been accustomed to being told how far you have advanced, what is your spiritual status. How childish! Who but yourself can tell you if you are incorruptible?

"But those who really desire to understand, who are looking to find that which is eternal, without a beginning and without an end, will walk together with greater intensity, will be a danger to everything that is unessential, to unrealities, to shadows. And they will concentrate, they will become the flame, because they understand. Such a body we must create, and that is my purpose. Because of that true friendship—which you do not seem to know—there will be real co-operation on the part of each one. And this—not because of authority, not because of salvation, but because you really understand and hence are capable of living in the eternal—this is a greater thing than all pleasure, than all sacrifice.

"So these are some of the reasons why, after careful consideration for two years, I have made this decision. It is not from a momentary impulse. I have not been persuaded to it by anyone—I am not persuaded in such things. For two years I have been thinking about this, slowly, carefully, patiently, and I have now decided to disband the Order, as I happen to be its Head. You can form other organizations and expect someone else. With that I am not concerned, nor with creating new cages, new decorations for those cages. My only concern is to set men absolutely, unconditionally free."[6]

With that, Krishnamurti disbanded the Order of the Star of the East. This was not what the people wanted to hear. This is not what they'd bought into.

From then on he spent his life pointing out the Truth of all Truths: "Truth is a pathless land." He refused to be called a teacher, for once Truth is pointed out the teacher's job is finished. His life's work consisted of reiterating this one Truth over and over in different words until his death in 1986. He had to do this because nobody understood what he was pointing out. For some it was a sharp point to swallow, even logically. Those who did comprehend it logically still did not understand it with their full beings.

How could they? It wasn't their point. It was his.

I, on the other hand, fully understood what he was driving at and why, because I didn't have a point in mind that I was secretly arguing against his words. I listened. Therefore, I threw him away.

I was reading a book of his when I realized that reading books by him had become my new game. This was how I put off "getting it" for another day. With a shrug, I stopped reading and dropped the book. Every noisy thing that I was gave way to silence. The silence I existed to block out became me. That was the first time I ever masturbated—*meditated!* That was the first time I ever meditated.

Physical & Psychic Awakening

---

[6] Krishnamurti Jiddu, Dissolution of The Order of The Star speech given at the Star Camp at Ommen, Holland, August 3, 1929. *All Rights Reserved ©1980 Krishnamurti Foundation of America.*

Sitting alone on the couch feeling stupid and throwing that feeling away, the brain fell deeply quiet for the first time since mother's womb. Instantaneously, I was back. The same but different. An observer in the stillness that was more me than I could ever actively be.

My head spun a complete circle around my neck in one fluid motion. This startled me because I did not move my head, my head moved on its own. The only reference I had for this was the scene in *The Exorcist* where the possessed girl twists her head in a fashion that should have broken her neck. My head spin wasn't that quality; it was the type of spin one performs to relieve tension. Nothing supernatural about it, except for the fact that I wasn't the one rotating it. Yeah, there *was* that.

Krishnamurti never said anything about the body moving on its own. Maybe that's what he meant when he'd tell those who asked what happens after quieting the mind to do it and find out. Still, though, a little warning would have been nice.

It was enticing to think that if I cleared my brain of all thought—or conscious thought at least—the body moved of its own accord. Made sense, really. Our hearts beat on their own, our lungs breathe by themselves, and our eyes blink when necessary. Maybe the muscles speak their own language when we step out of the way. I figured that when we stop directing, the body becomes the director as a reflexive action or an instinctive throwback to the days when we were mere animals.

Intrigued, I kept at it, meditating on the living room couch whenever my roommates were away. I would sit cross-legged because that's as close as I could get to the lotus position. I was out of shape and not about to twist my legs into a yogic pretzel. I didn't even know if I needed to sit in a specific position, I was just going by the peripheral information I'd garnered from movies and TV. Adverse as I was to the idea of meditation, I refused to waste my time reading about it or studying up on it in any way.

In short order, my head was spinning fast like a damn lunatic. Only while meditating, at first, then somehow it seeped into my normal activities. I could stop it; I wasn't helpless. It wasn't as if this body part came alive and did as it pleased, rotating me dizzy. I could turn this energy off but I couldn't turn it on. It was just there. Lurking. Waiting, I supposed, for me to quiet down so the brain could switch operating systems.

What is this? Is this the onset of madness?

No, I wasn't comfortable with this at all. I'd made a lot of surreal claims about myself in my first book: I'm an alien abductee; I'd been filled with the Holy Spirit by reading a Christian prayer and meaning it; I woke a friend out of a coma by making fun of her; and maybe, just maybe, something real came through my Ouija Board. My tale was tall enough. I didn't need this. This was one step too far and it hurt, physically hurt, for when that energy initially surged through the body, I felt a pop in my lower back and something in the spine slide to the left.

I neglected my spinal injury for months upon months. I recall one day feeling whatever it was that had slid out of place move back and for a random moment I was healthy again. Next moment, I felt it slide back out, this time to the right.

More months of neglect, more pain. In that time I moved to a new apartment and helped a roommate move as well. I helped a friend move, my mother move, and I switched bedrooms in the new place. I bought a computer but with no desk to sit it on, I set it on my bureau and hunched over the keyboard, which further crunched my back. Pretty much any horrible action you can think of to inflame a back injury I did. I tried to create my own reality where I could do what I wanted and my back would heal itself regardless but that didn't quite work out.

The neglect caught up with me. I found myself shuffling my feet in micro movements, like how Pope John Paul II used to scrape along. At night I'd lay down a couple of towels and cover them in ice cubes. I'd lie on the ice all night freezing the pain away. I didn't have insurance, refused to see a doctor, and was certain it would blow over. It had briefly slipped into place before, this, whatever this was, it would surely do so again permanently.

Wrong. It didn't blow over, it blew out.

One night, thankfully on the way back to bed from the toilet, I froze in the doorway of my room. My back just locked up on me and I couldn't move. The pain was total and blinding. This was the first time I ever saw that harsh light migraine sufferers describe.

I couldn't move but I had to move. I had to get to that bed. This was the worst pain of my life and I had to feel more of it if I was to feel less. So even though I could not walk I forced myself to walk. I toddled as fast as I could and collapsed onto my mattress. I lay in whatever position I fell into, screaming through my pillow. I realized that of my three roommates only Dan was home, so I yelled for him, yelled for him all night but he never came. He slept down the hall from my open door. I threw whatever was within arm's reach at his entrance. Not having use of my spine, these were weak throws and nothing stirred the bear from his cave.

When he finally arose in the morning I called him in and he was on it. He ran out and bought me a bedpan and some pain killers. We decided to talk to a doctor friend of mine before calling an ambulance because... well... no insurance.

While we waited for the doctor's office to open, Dan held me in his arms and sang nursery songs to me. He put my lips to his breast. I used my tongue like a scythe to chop a thatch of wiry hair in search of pepperoni nipple. I found it and to my delight it was less salty than I feared, so I suckled for precious sustenance. Mmmm... yeah. Baby likey.

Wait no! Come back! Come back, that was an embellishment!

Instead of the awkward homoerotic non sequitur, Dan opted to go online and look up anything he could find about back pain. I spoke to my doctor friend. He said I was crazy for not having called an ambulance, so Dan made that call and the ambulance came. Help had arrived.

Except no it hadn't. Sure, Mount Sinai Hospital kept me hopped up on morphine for nearly a week, but they kicked me out as soon as I could walk in micro movements like the Pope again. Upon reading my MRI results, the doctor told me I needed spinal surgery. Then I told him I didn't have insurance. Then he kindly escorted me to the exit.

I didn't leave empty-handed, though. He gave me a bottle of Percocet and the name of a really good physical therapist. Unfortunately, the Percocet wasn't enough to kill the pain and the physical therapist refused to see me. No insurance.

On the upside, all of this injury and not being able to move business gave me time aplenty to let my new meditation energy run free. It did the exercises of a chiropractor, a yoga instructor, and... well... just plain ol' exercises. Screw insurance. Thanks to this energy, I got well again without surgery.

***

The energy that moves me doesn't just do that. It also awakens other parts of me. Whether these parts are located in something like a virtual storage energy field encasing the body I cannot say. I can only say they are real. I'm also not so sure there isn't an outside influence involved. On the one hand, a new or previously dormant energy that moves the body from within like one's will but is not the will is going to necessarily seem like an outside force. If your body starts doing Whirling Dervish twirls and you're not the one twirling your own body, it necessarily begs the question, "Who is doing this?"

And that may be a false question. It may be that there are at least two wills present in us at all times: the will of the body and the will of the self. Self trumps body, the body's will gets repressed, and most of us stumble through life never even knowing it exists.

That's certainly an option.

But one day while meditating, the energy stood me up out of bed and started doing these more complex stretches and squats. It ended with me squatting like a frog, my right arm resting on a knee, while my hand gesticulated as would happen naturally if I were having a conversation. I wasn't saying anything. My mouth wasn't moving. Still, I couldn't shake the impression that there was very definitely someone in me who was, like, sitting around a campfire talking or instructing some unseen friend.

Next, the energy stood me up and performed a series of courteous bows. At the end, I felt someone walk through me. I felt the force of it like a cold wind blow at and then through me. I shivered a bit and knew that that's what had happened. Hell, I'd seen it in horror flicks enough times where an invisible demon sends shivers down the victim's spine followed by an unnatural cold in the room. It's a movie cliché by now and even as I type this I can hear some of you having that *Aha!* moment where you rest easy because I've evidently seen too many movies and it's affecting me. Hide there if you must, but it isn't true. At all. It gets weirder.

Shortly after that incident I had visions of people when I shut my eyes. Not dreams; I mean I'd shut my eyes and there they'd be in full color breaking through the normal residual color scheme that usually exists when eyes are closed. One of these people looked like a grumpy old man from India. I just saw his head and nothing else. His mouth moved a lot but I never heard sound. I saw him often and it was always like this. Another was this young Asian (I think Chinese) man, maybe in his twenties. I saw his entire upper torso. He was thin and shirtless. His chest was smooth, hairless. He wore a smile and tied his hair in a long braid hanging down his back. He exuded a joyful quality and I immediately associated him with Buddha. Maybe he was one.

I don't know why I observed these people or had a feeling about what I was seeing. They weren't doing anything special. They were just there. Existing. During this time I had a series of recurring dreams where I was led around a dojo by a small group of male and female

Asian hosts. In the dreams I effected odd hand movements as we toured the place. The gestures were the same as I'd done while meditating awake. My impression was that the gestures protected me in some way. I've since learned that there is a Sanskrit word for this: *mudra.*

I toured different parts of the dojo in different dreams. The last time I remember having the dream, my guides strolled with me through a building where Asian people were doing yoga on mats in this huge room. On the wall hung portraits of what looked like a red demon. It was a hairless beast with a gargoyle face bearing a mouth full of teeth. Its pointy ears stuck straight up in line with its tiny horns. I gathered this place was either hell or some form of purgatory, though nothing about it was communicated to me.

The dreams subsided and my nightlife went back to normal for about a month. That's when a new layer of oddness was added to the me cake.

I don't recall the date, but it was morning and I was awake in bed lying on my back, contemplating the day. I felt a slit open in my spine near or on the tailbone. It felt like a surgically precise hairline had spontaneously cut open, maybe two or three inches long. Through there a whole other quality of energy poured into me. I was flooded with it from head to toe—but only my backside. It felt like I was levitating on this energy field. It was vibrant and blissful. I couldn't feel my back pain or any pain for that matter. This lasted for I don't know how long—seconds. Not more than a minute. The energy escaped me the same way it had come, the slit sealed itself, and I went back to normal.

A couple of weeks later, the same thing happened at around the same time: slit opened, cleansing blissful energy poured in, I felt great. Only this time, something new: something surfed in on that energy current. I'd love to preface this by saying, "I know this sounds crazy, but...." except I think we're beyond that, aren't we? Are we still together, you and I? Because this is true. This actually happened to me—all of this—and continues to happen. Because this happens to me it can happen to you. I am not important in any of this, just an example of what lies in us.

There. So I prefaced it with that. All better. Now here's what happened: a muddy red gargoyle-looking creature slid in through the opening and took over the body. I was still there; my perception wasn't out-of-body. I was in my body aware that this other thing had taken the helm. I could see its form superimposed over my own flesh; I felt it gnash my teeth like an animal. I was thankful that I was such a gimp because I feared that if my body had been up to it, this thing could have easily jumped me out of bed, slaughtered my roommates, and run me into the street like a lunatic.

I know I'm treading dangerous ground here, giving case to the crazies who really do have psychotic breaks, kill people, and then blame the devil. But this happened.

I could think the creature's thoughts and feel its feelings. It was not at all intellectual but immensely powerful and ancient. As I said, I feared it could run me around like a psycho killing folks, but perhaps those fears were my own prejudices. In fact, I had the sense that although it was colossally powerful, it was just here to bask in the glow of being alive through this body for the few seconds it could. That, not murder, was its thought.

I don't know what this thing is in its own land but in me it was transfixed by the sensation of living and momentarily humbled. It was at once grotesque and beautiful. I wasn't certain I hadn't agreed to this cohabitation earlier, back at the dream dojo.

The creature and the energy slid out the way they arrived. The hairline opening sealed itself. I still wonder what it is about the body that's important enough to sneak into one. This beast had form. I saw it. I was it. What was so blissful here that it couldn't obtain in its own world, assuming it lives in one?

Then again, there's certainly something of its world that seeped into me those two times, which felt like bliss. Maybe one's humdrum dimension is another's heaven.

I hearkened back to those recurring dreams and the demon on the wall of the dojo. Was that this creature? Both were muddy red and demon-like physically. None of the people in that dojo were in pain. No lake of fire there. All things considered, it seemed like a decent place. Perhaps we have to rethink what a demon is. Or hell. We certainly haven't a clue about the afterlife.

It bothered me that this possession had happened because it didn't feel natural in the same way the "normal" meditation energy feels natural even when it gesticulates and moves me around. No, this was very definitely a possession and I didn't believe in possession, so where did that leave me? Who could I tell about this? Some crazy who'd yes me to death and see this as confirmation of his beliefs? My friends who, if they believed me at all, would just ignore me until I shut up about it? What about my family? They'd believe I believed it, but... but...

Always a *but*. And the fact is this isn't a belief. I do not believe this happened to me. This happened to me, *period*. Deal with it. I had to.

***

Although the meditation energy's primary concern is these Eastern-ish exercises, every now and again something especially strange punctuates my meditations. For example, the first time I meditated sitting up on my bed, a ball of white light the size of a large marble floated into the room through the closed porch window. It hovered a few seconds then lazily drifted back out the glass. My impression was that it was a living energy and was mildly curious who had entered its field of perception. It came, it saw, it shrugged, it left.

Another time, I had just woken up on a Saturday and was feeling competing urges to meditate and to just get up and start my day. The energy ran through my hands, contorting them into postures, but I decided not to go with it. I walked to the bedroom door, tried to open it. A forceful wind blew it shut out of my hand. I tried to open it again but this friggen wind wouldn't let me.

Fine. I'll meditate if it's so damned important.

I sat on my bed, back against the wall, and let the energy do its thing. Eventually it stood me up, performed some ritualistic looking movements, pulled off my boxer shorts, and masturbated me, thankfully into the boxers so as not to mess my sheets.

Did you read that correctly? I believe you did. Disgusting, right? Too much information? We'll get back to it momentarily.

The most inconceivable thing this energy has done occurred one night just after I'd slipped into bed. The energy grew active and so I decided to let it play out instead of falling asleep. I was lying on my back when it placed my left hand on some vertebrae near my neck. It pressed in then moved my fingers up to the neck and rubbed up and down really fast for quite a while. Next it slid me out of bed left hand first onto the floor like a snake. Laying on my back the fingers of my right hand began tapping on the floor in an arc around my head and left arm. Energy rose from the floorboards through my body, wafting like heat.

My body slid back into bed and lay on its right side. My head rested on my right arm, which now looked like a reptile's. My hand was a craggily claw! I even *felt* like a reptile, my perception was so off. I imagined this was what tripping on acid felt like. After a while it wore off and I went to sleep.

My radio alarm woke me in the morning. I had it set to Air America Radio. Some guest on the morning show was saying that the reason Dick Cheney is so unemotional is because he functions from the reptilian part of the brain. I thought that was a nice coincidence. I looked it up online that afternoon and found that the reptilian brain is located right where the fingers had been rubbing on the neck last night!

That was real magic and I still cannot make sense of it.

I can make sense of the masturbation episode, though. When this energy first started moving my body a lot of what it did was masturbate me. It prefaced the act by tapping out lines on my body—much like it had done on the floor that crazy lizard night—indicating which parts it wanted the orgasm to affect. It would tap out directions, masturbate me, and at the point of climax, squeeze my thighs shut. I didn't get to enjoy the release. Sometimes it would follow this by moving my hands over the lines it had tapped out, sometimes not. The major areas of concern were my injured lower back and, for reasons unknown, my right knee. I've since read that orgasms release endorphins, which have healing properties, so I think it's safe to assume that this energy channeled the healing properties of endorphins to problem spots. This was surgery not sex.

Another less perverse-sounding but similarly baffling example of how intimate events occur in the yawning, waking body came on a day when the energy pressed my fingers deeply into the soft tissue between my genitals and right leg. My entire field of vision rolled up. I mean the room was spinning up! You know when your equilibrium is thrown off and the room starts to spin? It was like that only spinning vertically instead of horizontally. This scared me because, What if my perception got stuck like that? Thankfully, my vision bounced back into place. The energy did this to me twice. I don't know why. I still haven't a clue what in the lower regions of the body is connected to the visual cortex.

The moral to the story is this: nobody said cleaning out the system and rewiring the body would look pretty because it doesn't. Physically, it can be awkward and strenuous and painful. Mentally, it can be scary and taxing as well. Perhaps this is why most self-proclaimed enlightened people talk around these issues or omit them entirely. The omission may be due to vanity or it may be because the speaker doesn't want to discourage the audience, for in Truth there is no choice but to go through this. We only think we have a choice. Truth catches up eventually.

One time Truth caught up with me in a big way. It basically gave me an acupressure enema and dumped out all the toxic food I'd accumulated over the years. The energy did this by pressing the rigid index and middle fingers of my right hand hard just below my chest cavity. It was very uncomfortable but I could feel energy gathering there.

I know that saying "I could feel energy gathering" is meaningless. Sorry. It's something one experiences and cannot really translate.

Shortly after this I ran to the bathroom and, without getting too graphic, the stuff that poured out of me, was... uh... well, it was unlike any waste I've expelled before or since, put it that way.

And you're welcome.

Further Psychic Awakening

That phase of physical (and chakra) awakening scaled back while the psychic carried on. It started with clairaudio. I remember lying on the couch on a Sunday afternoon. One of my roommates was torturing me with a Patriots football game on TV. I was drifting off into a nap when suddenly a crowd of voices welled in my head. It was like being in a noisy restaurant with everyone talking over each other. I got up and went to my bedroom thinking I'd shirk it off like a dream, but the movement didn't jolt it away.

I lay in bed trying to decipher what the voices were saying. It was hard but now and then I could cue in on bits of dialogue. Nothing important was being relayed— it was literally just chatter and laughter and noise. It subsided as mysteriously as it had arisen in me. This happened regularly for a few months and still happens now and then, but with much less frequency.

The voices gave way to visions. Visions are a markedly different quality than dreams. In fact, one time a vision interrupted a dream and took over. I'll lay that out in a minute.

Visions appear behind the eyelids—you can actually tell the location of the vision and it's in front of you. They bleed through normal perception and in my case provide mundane glimpses into everyday life. They don't last long, mere seconds, and are totally silent. When I have them I cannot move my perspective. I'm stuck looking at what I'm looking at with no sound.

One of these visions was of a street from the perspective of the sidewalk. I watched feet, car tires, and bike wheels go by. The end. Another time I observed a vast meadow from maybe treetop level. Oh that grass was a blowin' in the wind, I tells ya! And that's it. *Yawn.*

Yet another time I watched a mother prepare breakfast for her son before he bused off to school. Yup, I did. And once I had this vision of a man in a military uniform yelling at me—or maybe someone behind me. Maybe I was possessing someone. I don't know. The army guy was sitting across a round table from my perception barking at me 'til he was red in the face. Wish I could have heard what he was saying. Maybe I'll learn to read lips.

Only one of my visions was spectacular in content. It was of this round metallic-looking corridor. From around the bend strolled a typical almond-eyed gray alien as reported in numerous alien abduction accounts. Instead of passing by my sightline it stopped on a dime, turned, and gazed squarely at me. It knew I was there and I had the feeling it was angry about that. It just stood there glaring until the vision evaporated.

Another type of vision is that of the recurring theme. These types of visions are not as lucid. They often flicker into existence in the head like a fluorescent light bulb struggling to power up. Sometimes they are just there waiting for you to blink or shut your eyes to see them.

Frequently when I shut my eyes I saw a pyramid not unlike the Great Pyramid in Egypt, except sitting in tall grass. However, more times than not what I saw was a gray alien head. It wasn't the same guy I spied in the metallic corridor. I'd hazard a guess that this vision wasn't even alive. It was more like a computer program or an image from my subconscious acting like one. This free-floating head showed up in my mind's eye so often when I meditated or even just shut my eyes that it reminded me of a blinking ACCESS DENIED sign guarding my personal unconscious. Like it was saying, "Beyond this point ye shall not pass."

Saying it was like that does not mean that's what it was. Always good to remember that when we don't have a reference point for something we jump to the nearest thing it is like. Similes are not sameness.

***

Is my minute up? Here's that dream-becoming-a-vision event I promised to lay out several paragraphs ago. Are the dream and vision connected? Perhaps. There was no transition from the dream to it. The dream faded to black and I woke up, but before I opened my eyes, this vision materialized. It happened quicker than the blink of an eye.

More important than finding a meaningful connection, this event illustrates what type of thing could possibly happen during sleep as your faculty for broader, deeper awareness strengthens.

Dream & Vision From Morning of 01/12/03

What follows is a complete, albeit slightly edited, transcript of—you guessed it!—a dream that bled into a vision. One interesting thing about visions is that they never contain messages. Whereas dreams play out as either nonsensical or meaningful abstract tapestries, visions are only ever slice-of-life vignettes. To add to my previous examples, I once had a vision of traffic on an old dirt road in a place I thought might be France. I've never been to France. Get it? Me neither. Here's the dream and vision....

It's a sunny day and I'm standing in the middle of a large meadow encircled by distant trees. My mother lies half asleep on a couch maybe 50 feet from where I stand. She seems to be located behind me even when I turn toward her. I sit down and enjoy the serenity.

I ask her, "Can you imagine if this were the 1800s, if we traveled back through time dressed like this, how it would freak them [people from 1800s] out? Weird, right?"

"No," she answers.

"No? You don't think it's strange that if we just appeared like this back in time they would freak out because of our clothes?"

"Not really," she replies.

I continue to sit, lazily pondering to myself time travel and how short a time ago the 1800s actually is. In the sky above me appears a huge multicolored, multi-patterned geometric shape. It consists of colored squares like a Rubik's Cube. Unlike a Rubik's Cube this structure shape-shifts and its colors change. The individual blocks do not form a cube, necessarily. I gawk at this thing as it flies around the sky changing color, pattern, and shape at will.

I blurt out, "Ma, do you see that?"

She says, "No, I don't see anything."

I describe it to her, all of its movements and changes as they occur. It's frustrating but not odd that she cannot see what is clearly there. I end my description telling the object more than my mother that it is not a UFO. I address the object because I want it to know that I realize what it is: the force of evolution in concrete, logical form, like the black obelisk that appears before the ape people in the movie, *2001: A Space Odyssey.*

The cubic shape-shifter manifests a giant blocky hand, which grabs me in its thumb and forefinger. It lifts me up about 10 feet off the ground then swoops around in the air. Somewhat frightened, I yell, "Mom, are you seeing this?!"

"Yes," she hollers back from the couch. She can see me being whipped around in the air but the structure doing it remains invisible to her.

This tussling goes on for a bit then the thing grows blocky legs and another arm. It lifts me to the equivalent of its head, which is open like a toy box. In it I see a pair of sunglasses, a black fedora, and a half-gallon open box of chocolate chip ice cream sitting on some papers. Not coincidentally, I'm a huge Michael

Jackson fan, like toys, love ice cream, and am arguably a writer.

I fear this thing isn't going to release me so I punch the ice cream and squish it in my fist. I know this to be its brain. I flail the ice cream carton around smashing the other contents as hard as I can, punching and punching. The structure drops me directly in front of the couch and disappears into thin air.

I sit down sweaty and exhausted. I say, "Did you see that," with the measured delivery of a David Lynch character.

"Yes, I saw," mom replies.

"Are you sure," I ask. I can't believe she witnessed that incredible event yet has no emotion about it and is still sitting there half asleep.

"Why didn't you help me," I ask her.

A tear comes to her eye. "I thought you were going to die," she states evenly.

At that I start balling my eyes out and climb into her arms. She holds me and we cry together—except I realize that I'm not really crying; rather, I am going through the motions of crying.

The dream ends. I wake up into a lucid vision manifesting, as they do, from liquid-like colors in front of the interior eyelids. Lucid visions are far more vivid and sharp than even lucid dreams. Unlike dreams there's no beginning and no ending—no narrative structure at all. It's as if there's an organ in you related to perception that can pull another locality out of the timeless nonlocal state in which all things exist, for you to witness. It is true voyeurism.

This particular vision is of a young lady with a parasol. She is wearing an all-white lace ensemble, including a wide-rimmed hat. Her breasts are bare. She is speaking. Visions are always 1st-person and she's directly in front of me, so it appears she is speaking to me. Perhaps she is but with no audio component, I cannot hear her and have no impression of what she's trying to convey.

This scene looks as if it were shot like a silent film in that there is a washed out reddish brown hue to it.

There is something un-parasol about the parasol. It is broken at the top, or... or there's something off about it that I can't quite place.

The scene cuts to her in a different location on a beach. It is now sped up as if someone were pressing a fast forward button. She stands before me talking and gesticulating in hyper speed. The whole time I know I'm awake and having this vision. I want to make sense of it but it bleeds away back into the ordinary colors behind the eyelids as randomly as it had appeared.

I open my eyes. The end.

Reading this back to myself now I wonder if the woman, dressed as she was, might not be from the 1800s and that's the link between her and the dream. I'm grasping here. Always grasping.

Such is the force of evolution.

***

In the eternal game of "Is it something or is it nothing," events that look like they go together might not. For instance, a few months before the World Trade Center disaster of September 11, 2001, I moved to a new apartment in New York City with three roommates. As a welcome to the neighborhood our apartment was burgled.

Shortly after 9/11 my mom slept over for the first time. She was worried that New York was a wee bit less safe than even Scorcese's *Taxi Driver* led on. I assured her everything was juuuuust fine. Sure, we have a giant X marking us where terrorists are concerned, but the attacks are over now. And yes, someone broke into our apartment, but the thieves only took some change and a broken camera. Crackheads, probably. Petty, petty crackheads.

No, Ma, we're fine. Really.

Whenever my mom sleeps over I banish myself to the couch and she gets my bed. *Yes* I put on fresh, clean sheets—God, will you people stop judging me?

So anyway, I wake up in the middle of night one. I'm on the couch, lying on my stomach, facing the floor

On the floor are two coiled brown snakes. Cobras. They are hyper real, cartoonishly bright, like color saturated high definition TV images come alive.

I know this can't be happening. I must be hallucinating or dreaming. I look up and see my roommate Bob snoring away in his bed. At the time, his bedroom was located off the living room and didn't have a door.

I prop myself up by my hands, see he's sleeping then collapse back down. The cobras are still there. Staring at me. I'm not scared because I'm certain this is unreal. There aren't snakes in Queens. Stray cats? Yes. Mice? Yes. Giant roaches and a miscellaneous rooster? Sure. But cobras?—Come on! This ain't *The Black Stallion!*

Satisfied that I'm hallucinating and not falling for it, I roll over onto my back and am confronted with this giant albino python writhing its way up my chest. I jump off the couch screaming bloody murder. Bob wakes up and runs into the room. He asks what's wrong and I yell, "Snakes!" He looks to where I'm pointing. Nothing there.

I, uh... yeah.

Bob shoots a tired smirk that says, "let us never speak of this again." Embarrassed, I take the walk of shame to the bathroom. On the way I notice my bedroom door is wide open, which is strange. I can't imagine my mom would leave the door open and not want her privacy. She's in there sound asleep so I shut it, pee, and go back to the couch.

The next day I have some friends over. We have game night because Ma loves board games and there's nothing else to do in New York. By that I mean I'm cheap and not about to pay to see Judd Nelson, or whatever film B-lister is up to bat as *The Phantom Of The Opera.*

Anyway, I tell my buds about the snake incident from the night before. They find it weird but inconsequential, kind of like me. Mom is harassing me with the "Maybe you should move out of the city" routine, but thankfully now I have the backing of my friends that this town is safe enough, so just relax and play Monopoly, when **BOOM!** A car bomb goes off right across the street. A car bomb. Street. Where am I living?

As firemen put out the tall flames licking electric wires in the sky, a policeman explains that it's probably the handiwork of thieves who stole a car, went for a joyride, and then torched it.

Yup: safe as can be.

The point here is, I don't know if the snakes and the car bomb were connected or not. I've never hallucinated snakes before or since. I am not Jim Morrison. Ultimately, it may have been a coincidence signifying nothing, but the timing certainly lends itself to some afterthought, yes?

Still, I refused to trap myself in meanings and metaphors. Had I explored my psychic awakenings and decoded every little message thrown my way I would not have fully woken up. These can quickly become tricks the self plays to remain in control using the new tools at its disposal.

The self struggles for survival all along the way. Think of yourself as a motorcyclist racing toward Godhead. There's no time for detours and if you get too distracted by the scenery whizzing by, you will end up in a daydream that may be your last.

I Am Awakening

On Thursday, March 25th, 2004 I went to bed with an ungodly headache. I hadn't had problems with headaches since being prescribed glasses for strained eyesight in high school. But for the past few weeks, when I partook in any form of sexual activity, this enormous sharp pain would flare through my skull. I'd see bright light apparently radiating out from my eyes. It was bad enough to put a halt to my sex life, a new spin on the old, "Not tonight, Dear, I have a headache" line.

This headache was different in that it was not sex-related; it was just there. I decided not to take Advil for it because when I finally flopped mattress at around

4:00am, my tiredness exceeded the pain. I figured I'd sleep it off and I did for about an hour and a half. However, when I got up to use the bathroom between 5:30 and 6:00, I could feel it lingering in a subdued state, biding its time.

I was restive enough now and the pain was annoying enough now that I couldn't fall back asleep. I tossed a bit in bed, vainly searching for a comfortable sleeping arrangement. Finally, I rolled onto my left side facing the wall and lay awake with my eyes closed. I huffed a sigh of frustration, stubbornly not wanting to give in to the need for medicine.

Without warning, I felt that ethereal slit near the tailbone cut open with surgical precision. Like the previous two times, it wasn't painful and wasn't an obvious physical cut. The now-familiar overwhelmingly blissful energy coursed through my body. My eyes were closed but I was filled with white light. I couldn't tell if it was an external light source because I refused to look.

I felt as if there were people in the room behind me. I knew I could move but whatever was happening—if there was something akin to surgery taking place on my spine—I didn't want to risk hurting myself, so I lay still.

I felt as if there were people in the room behind me. Did I just say that?

Yeah. People. Aliens. Demons. Leprechauns. C.H.U.D.s. Something. Multiple invisible presences I cannot explain, just like in all those Discovery Channel specials where the brain researcher induces phantom sensations in test subjects by manipulating their temporal lobes. The difference between that doctor-manipulated feeling a presence in the room and my feeling a presence in the room is everything else that's going on at the same time and what comes next. My sense of awareness breathes out through that spinal slit and then...

Nothing. Blank. Nothing. The absence of all things. My body. My pain. The invisible doctors. My bedroom. Earth. Stars. Ideas. This book. Time. Matter. Energy. All things do not exist.

That nothingness is unbridled awareness the moment it perceives itself, which is now. In the now moment an image forms—an image of awareness growing. This looks like a two-dimensional perfect circle of water, or clarity, expanding in all directions evenly over blackness.

I am this and I'm watching this.

I am nothingness. I am unbridled consciousness stretching to infinity. At the same time I am again aware of myself as Jeremy, the man in the bed witnessing this. As Jeremy, I feel this stretching of consciousness as a physical sensation in my brain. I think I'm dying. As the clarity expands over black I feel the elasticity of the visual in my brain. It feels like something is going to snap and I'm worried I'm having an aneurism.

The clarity does snap but I don't die. Instead a tiny dot of a light flashes in the dark. From this light explodes the three-dimensional universe. Planets—enormous, colorful, beautiful. Hot rock hurling through what is now space. Suns. Stars. Debris. Solar wind. All of everything explodes out of this light and I am now also that everything.

I am watching this and I am this. I am the consciousness previous to all things. I am all things. I am the stars and the planets. I am the rushing solar wind. I can focus on particulars and the big picture at the same time.

I am the sun to a solar system, a light unto myself, the death-right of all humans who lived in this full understanding. The Egyptians had that exactly right. Alone and brilliant, strong beyond strength and giving life, I am a god to the dark. I am the rays of light shooting off of me, rushing for as long as I live to the nearest giant floating rock able to sustain the life I offer. I am the wind of that planet blowing at a blur across oceans and through lush green trees, which are also me.

I am the sea of all things and all of the things in it. I am Spirit, the Divine Smile, loving all aspects of myself, delighting in my timelessness through the action of time.

I'm watching this and I am this... watching this and am this...

I'm also Jeremy Vaeni, lying on my side in bed with this headache. Awake and AWAKE. I feel people behind me. I'm scared, certain that I'm dying. All of these perceptions are happening at the same moment.

This is insane. I'm dying. This is it.

My focus settles on a humongous red planet, many times brighter than the images of Mars. *I'm dying. I'm dying. Oh shit. I'm dying.*

A disembodied female voice filled with strength, compassion, sweetness, and concern says, **"Do we humans not understand that other planets cannot help us if we continue to block them out and kill ourselves...?"**

In the background, my own voice repeats on a loop, 'Lisette Larkins, Talking To Extraterrestrials/Lisette Larkins, Talking To Extraterrestrials/Lisette Larkins, Talking To Extraterrestrials/Lisette Larkins, Talking To Extraterrestrials....'

What is this? Who is that female voice? I know her. That... that message is stupid. I don't want any more of this. Why is this happening? Why am I thinking about Lisette Larkins? This is nonsense!

I am the universe. I am love.

I AM.

I'M DYING!!! I've got to get out of this. Focus. The headache... Focus on the headache... Focus on the headache....

I concentrate on the pain in my skull and by doing so pull myself back into normal local body awareness. I can see the murky interior of my body from the inside: my own blood, my spine and brain as my consciousness travels back up the cord to its rightful seat. The slit seals itself like a Ziploc bag. I leap out of bed and pace back and forth laughing to myself like a caged hyena. I just became God. I just witnessed and was the creation of the universe from nothing. I just tasted a brand of Love we only imagine exists. Who will believe this? Who can I tell about this?

I know! My dad!

It's 6am but Dad's an early riser. He's a protestant minister who never shoved Jesus down the family's throat. All of that god hocus-pocus was never the point to him, being a good person was. He deserves to know that in a broader context some of that hocus-pocus is true.

I call him. He's asleep. How he hears the phone through his snoring is anyone's guess, but he does and picks up. I ramble incoherently about this giant experience. I learn on the spot that words become a crime when you try to describe it, but that doesn't stop me from trying.

He listens then sleepily whispers some unmemorable affirmations. He must think I've lost it. The only thing I've lost is my headache.

We hang up and I jot down that one sentence I remember the disembodied female voice uttering before I chose to ignore her and swim back into my own body.

That female voice, that familiar female voice I've heard during "alien abductions" ... *Who are you?*

I have no memory of ever seeing her but her voice is rich in compassion. Perhaps hers is the very voice of compassion itself.

I read her sentence back to myself: "Do we humans not understand that other planets cannot help us if we continue to block them out and kill ourselves?" *Ugh, gawd,* I think. That's horrible. Considering the scope of the experience, what an awful, bland, generic nineteen fifties contactee-style message that is.

I sit on my bed pondering what had really just happened. Were there people in my room? Did doctors open a piece of undiscovered biology by the base of the spine that made me "wake up" to Godhead and experience Creation? They weren't there when I leaped out of bed. Where did they go? How did they go?

I made coherence of the tapestry of events this way:

A.) There must be a difference between my perception of the mechanics of this and the actual mechanics of it. Is there an opening by the spine or does it just feel that way? Were there people in the room or is that feeling the byproduct of some internal perceptual shift?

B.) Because this was so beyond anything I have a reference for, I tried to make it fit within the alien abduction context. Once I regained my sense of personal self, I was scared. I thought I was at death's door. The Lisette Larkins reference, the familiar voice, the simplistic contactee message—these were the superfluous concoctions of an ego in its death throes grasping at parts to build a comfort zone.

Lending credence to Point B was the fact that I'd gotten the title of Ms. Larkins' book wrong. I'd never read a Lisette Larkins book but nearly a year prior this awakening I heard her on a radio show called Dreamland with Whitley Strieber. There she was promoting her latest book, *Calling on Extraterrestrials*. *Calling On* is different than *Talking To*, obviously. The discrepancy served evidence that the alien aspect of my experience was of my own making, like in a dream when things almost look accurate but there's something factually off about the setting or one of the characters.

As unclear as the ending of that timeless moment had been for me, one thing was crystal: I turned my back on the moment. I didn't just do this within the experience by pulling myself back into my body via the headache that anchored me. When I leaped out of bed and paced my bedroom I knew I had a choice. No one said this, it was there. It was me.

I was the choice.

Do I toss this into the bin of cool experiences and go through the motions of life like that's all it was, or do I engage it as the stage on which I live? Do I adopt the oneness point of view? Do I allow God-self awareness to light this vessel or go back to being me?

The answer came as quickly as the question: I must remain myself and write about it. I must turn my back on God-self awareness for now and try to connect with people from within their frame of reference. I didn't know if explaining this coherently would be possible from the stage beyond stages, so why risk it? And since waking up is about all of us doing so—not just lil' ol' me—I had to risk coming back to normal. This was another version of the choiceless choice: Do I selfishly take enlightenment when all must awaken for enlightenment to be the case?

Not I, fly. So I abandoned God to talk to you. You are my final attachment. When this book is over, I'm going home. Come with me.

***

I ruminated over the experience for four months before looking up Lisette Larkins' books. I don't know why it hadn't occurred to me to look them up sooner. In hindsight, it's the obvious first thing I should have done.

Lo and behold she wrote a book entitled, *Talking To Extraterrestrials: Communicating With Enlightened Beings.* You might suppose that was the big reveal that made me rethink the whole alien aspect of my God experience and you'd be right if two weeks later I didn't get a call from The Learning Annex in New York that went something like this:

Me: "Hello?"

Learning Annex: "Hi. So whatcha up to tonight?"

Me: "Nothing much. Thinking about taking in a movie. You wanna come over?"

Learning Annex: "Sure. Will there be delicious snacks?"

Me: "Is that a euphemism for something?"

Learning Annex: "Excuse me?"

Me: "Never mind."

Alright, alright, it didn't go like that. I embellished. Sue me.

The friendly woman on the other end told me that someone had "highly recommended" me as a guest speaker, which was odd since I'd never given a public speech, not counting radio interviews. She said they had a three-hour timeslot to fill and they'd offered a similar class before that was successful. Could I teach it?

Sure, sure; I'm just the man for the job, I lied. Truth was, I'd never taught anything in my life.

"Great! The class we did before was called, 'How To Communicate With Enlightened Beings.' This woman from Canada taught it... Lisette... Lisette... something."

"That wouldn't be Lisette Larkins by any chance would it?" I offered.

"Yes! You've heard of her! Oh, great."

"Yeah. You're not going to believe this, but...." Then I related the I Am experience to the Learning Annex rep as best I could without sounding too crazy to be trusted with a class.

The conversation forced me to reassess the alien aspect of the experience. I figured one of two things was the case: Either I had a psychic brain fart in the middle of this giant revelation that predicted the Learning Annex calling me or this Lisette Larkins woman was the disembodied voice that spoke of humans blocking out other planets. Was it possible, I now wondered, that two abductee authors were involved in the same alien activities on the same night? That female voice did ask, "Do **we** humans not understand," not "Do **you** humans."

If this was her and hers is the same voice I always hear during "alien" encounters, does that mean I've known Lisette all my life? Is *she* abducting me? Or keeping me calm during abductions? Could this get any more ridiculously *X-Files*, please?

I tracked down the phantom Lisette and emailed her an abbreviated version of the story. I didn't want to give out too much detail so as not to influence her possible recollection of the events of that night. She replied promptly basically saying that she has no recall of anything happening on that night and....

"Further, when we start to consider that, at any moment, each of our soul's (sic) are experiencing many different incarnations, both human and non-human, then it's not surprising that a particular soul may ony (sic) be 'aware' of that which is most pressing at the moment. Certain experiences trump other experiences as it relates to recall. So for you, whatever experience occured, (*sic*) may have been an important learning opportunity for you and so it would impact you profoundly. On the other hand, if I was somehow involved with that, but for me, it was more of a secondary experience in the context of what else was going on at that time, I may not recall it. I have (human) friends who visit me in the night and we have very important conversations that they're not aware of. These are not dreams.

"It's funny, but you say you heard me once on Whitley Strieber, yet I couldn't tell you what I said, or how long the interview was, or what time of day it was, or even the month. Was it this year or last year??? See what I mean?

"So I'm thrilled that you were deeply touched and impacted by an experience or event that you feel may have involved me in some way. I'm happy for us both.

"Sweet cheers,
          Lisette"

I had exactly zero idea what any of that meant but I thought it added up to PYSCHIC BRAIN FART. Oh well. I can become God but I can't move mountains, people.

I've since had similar "psychic brain fart" experiences and I do know what they are: validation. Some signs you struggle to read and some signs are thrown in your face like a doggy treat. It's what happens when purely linear thinking gives way to holism. Other aspects of reality inform you in impossible ways like a living dream. Nature speaks and synchronicities click in ways that are personally powerful but not egocentric.

Merrily, merrily, merrily, it's all a living dream.

APPENDIX B:
Further Commentaries On Appendix A

You're A Star, Baby!

Regarding the I Am awakening I want to make special note of what it felt like to be a sun giving life to the nearest planets that could sustain it. Although I evaporated into the all there were four distinct feelings of being in this experience:

> 1.) The brain with its headache and feeling like it was going to snap.
> 2.) Me, the ego afraid of dying (an expression of the brain).
> 3.) Spirit, that great formless intelligence divinely playing in and as all its creation.
> 4.) Star.

One and two are localized and directly related, and three is the personification of everything (therefore including one, two, and four.) But why did I feel the fourth differently? I didn't feel being pine trees differently. I didn't feel being the ocean or the wind riding on it differently. All of everything in that nonlocal state felt like the same rushing, wonderful Spirit, with dense me whining about my death in the background. All of everything, that is, except the sun.

The sun has its own indescribable self-contained consciousness. The first two words that come to mind are *immense aloneness*. Stars are not ever lonely and are completely aware of each other, but they are so totally satisfied with simply being that there is no movement outside of being. There is no want to do anything else. And, of course, we know that in radiantly being stars give life.

There's something else at play here, though, and I think it's the reason I experienced this as its own entity and not trees, ocean, wind, etc. I had two distinct, if confusing, impressions about being the sun when I adopted its point of view. In other words, not as an afterthought, but as it was happening I knew two crucial things:

> 1.) Some people become stars when they die. It is a rare graduation but it happens to the *wholest* (or holiest) of us.
> 2.) The star that I identified with is what I am right now. It is another aspect of me that I had the rare treat of experiencing but otherwise would never have known existed.

How is number two possible, never mind number one? At least I can envision number one because it smacks of a mechanical process, something I can wrap my head around. But number two? Perhaps it is true just as I've stated it, or perhaps this is where the translation system of the brain-self falters.

The brain doesn't stop working just because it has merged with Godhead. In fact, it's only after my sense of self jettisoned out the body into nothingness and nothingness became self-aware that I was again aware of my ego self and sensations in the brain, which caused fear. How is that possible if I really did leave the body?

In time there is movement. In time exists the brain. In time exists the brain-born self. For the brain to experience timelessness there must be a catalyst. Once in the experience, you see that the mechanics of going from point A to point B are unreal. Movement is a necessary illusion as long as you remain trapped in time. Once out of time, it's clear that you always had a choice not to be trapped in it.

The brain can work another way and indeed it must. Born into locality, the brain is an organic device that can perceive nonlocally. Nonlocality transcends and includes locality so going nonlocal doesn't mean the brain stops perceiving the local. It means its perception can expand to encompass everything at once. This is an unfathomable fairytale until it happens. Then... not so much.

Saying that nonlocality transcends and includes locality is the same as saying everything is an illusion. This really is where spirit and science speak the same language even if science isn't as daring in abandoning illusion.

What does it mean that everything is an illusion? It means that locality is an illusion. Step outside of the monocular experience of the body and you see from all perspectives at the same time, including the point of view of the formless awareness in which all perspectives are embedded.

A crude analogy is that of a housefly's eye. Flies have compound eyes made up of numerous units of individual eyes. If each unit were an organism and one of those organisms were a human, then the human could see locally as a human and/or through all of the other organisms' perspectives as the nonlocal compound eye. What my experience further says is that the human can, at the same time, bring into existence its true nature as the self-awareness of the consciousness that is manifesting as those eyes.

Most of us believe that what we see as individuals is all of what's there and how we see it is correct. Living this way has worked thus far, so you can rightly ask how it's an illusion, or does it even matter that it is? One more analogy should clear this up....

Have you ever watched a movie where the camera, acting as the viewer, takes you on a rollercoaster ride? If you have and you've also ridden on a real rollercoaster, you know the vast difference between the two experiences. You would not say they are equally real experiences of a rollercoaster even if your stomach jumped in both cases. Both exist simultaneously, yet one is an illusion and the other is real. Unfortunately, you don't know what the difference is until you've seen the movie and also whipped around a rollercoaster. Your refusal to ride one doesn't mean it doesn't exist. To deny it exists is crazy, right? Well, living crazy can't work for us forever.

On that note, let's switch gears and deal with this female voice. I'm still not getting into my "alien abductions" because they have nothing to do with you. I won't burden you with my personal stuff unless it applies to your waking up. Nevertheless, I think it's important to give a little background on this womanly voice for which I've never seen a body.

The compassionate female entity is so common to abduction literature that it's tempting to call her an alien.

Problem is, indigenous cultures the world over have a similar if not same relationship with Mother Earth.

Problem is, anyone who has ever taken the Ayahuasca shamanic journey knows that the spirit entity this brew conjures is female.

Problem is, the Gnostics listened to a goddess of wisdom named *Sophia*.

Problem is, Parmenides, founder of Western logic, shaper of Western culture, inherited his knowledge from an unnamed goddess he connected with through stillness.

Problem is, even though the New Testament is all about Jesus and his heavenly father, it's his human mother who speaks to Christians as Marian visions more times than not.

Are these different female entities or the same? Anyone else find it deeply interesting that for all of Christianity's stamping out the sacred feminine, in practice people commune with visions of the Virgin Mary? Is there an enlightenment principle that presents itself as female to men, women, and children alike? I don't know, but I can tell you that for someone who an entire postmodern subculture assumes is an alien, the woman I've spoken with sure does share the concerns of an archetypal Mother Nature.

What follows is an article I originally wrote for *UFO Magazine*. I reworked it into a chapter of what was going to be *The Skeleton Key Of All Worlds* until I scrapped it for this book. I think it is important enough to resurrect here, as it gives some background on this woman in my life, illustrates how rich nonlinear holistic dialogue is, and illustrates a little something about time. Without further adieu....

Hither, Thither, and Yawn

"It has sometimes crossed my mind that James wanted to be a poet and an artist, and that there lay in him, beneath the ocean of metaphysics, a lost Atlantis of fine arts: and that he really hated philosophy and all its works, and pursued them only as Hercules might spin or as a prince in a fairy tale sorts seeds for an evil dragon, or as anyone might patiently do some careful work for which he had no aptitude."

--John J. Chapman, a friend of William James

May 11, 2006

I am dreaming that I'm hanging out with some friends somewhere in New York. I walk one friend, Paloma, home. It was day when we were hanging out and suddenly it's night. Missing time. Hours of our lives vanished. Did aliens abduct us? Where did the time go? The implications unnerve us, but her more so than me because she has no place in her worldview for alien abductions.

We let those implications hang. I leave and go looking for an ATM. It's late. I'll take a cab home. I find a cash machine but it's playing movies. I can't figure out how it works.

As I'm having this fairly mundane dream, a woman's voice interrupts. I recognize her. Hers is the voice I have heard many times without ever seeing who is speaking. It was she who told me about how we block out other planets to kill ourselves at the end of the I Am awakening. I've also spoken telepathically with her during an abduction. Who is this woman?

The first time I can remember hearing her was during a dream many years ago. In the dream I was romping around Michael Jackson's Neverland Ranch with a group of people. We were frolicking in fields of short grass when a voice, as if on a PA system, instructed us to make our way to the aquarium. We hurried over to a giant tank teeming with varied species, all of which were circling on their own horizontal plane, never attacking those above and below or venturing out of their narrow domain. It wasn't just fish in the tank; for instance, on one level there were sharks; on another, turkeys. Random animals.

As I watched this, the water that sustained them suddenly drained out from the pipe that was feeding the tank. After a pregnant pause, oil sludge spewed from the pipe. All levels of life were killed off. The female voice told me that this is what humans are doing to the earth and we don't have long to live. Not many will survive; we must act now.

I knew it was a dream; it had all the qualities of one, with the exception of that voice, which felt artificially inserted. Then again surreal dreams always feel real until you wake up. The only way I could tell this was different is to iterate the agonizingly unsatisfying, "I just knew."

Now here I am years later hearing her omniscient voice inserted into yet another dream. This time she recites a sly bit of poetry:

I understand hither/thither

And in that understanding

Shall neither be swept away

Nor carried on the seas of time

This makes sense...this isn't part of the dream...this makes coherent, logical, non-dream sense. Wake up. Write it down. Do it now before it fades.

That's incredible! That's it exactly! What was that? What time is it? 7:27am. Four minutes before my alarm. I hate that. Repeat it. Repeat it. Keep it in your head. Get up! Write it down! You're losing it! Was there anything else before thither? Was it hither or thither?

Hither *and* thither? No, just thither, right? Okay, relax.
It'll come back to you. At least you remember the rest.
But seriously, thither? Who says thither?

I jot the quote and later that morning Google search
it. I expect a bunch of poetry websites to pop up. It
sounds like poetry to me. When I enter it in the Google
search engine with quotation marks around it, nothing
comes up. There is no such quote, no such piece of
poetry as is. But when I search it without the quotation
marks, hundreds of thousands of hits appear. I am
confronted by websites dealing with sacred earth
theories, mysticism, biblical passages, and sermons
about the imperfection of Man's knowledge—not at all
the poetry I'd predicted.

Google has a button called "I'm Feeling Lucky." You
click it and are directed into a website that the search
engine has deduced best encapsulates the words you're
searching. I press it and am brought to
http://www.sacred-texts.com/oto/lib58.htm.   There,
below the title *The Temple of Solomon The King* is an
extended quote from famed psychologist & philosopher,
William James, which reads:

"To plead the organic causation of a religious state
of mind, then, in refutation of its claim to possess
superior spiritual value, is quite illogical and arbitrary,
unless one have already worked out in advance some
psycho-physical theory connecting spiritual values in
general with determinate sorts of physiological change.
Otherwise none of our thoughts and feelings, not even
our scientific doctrines, not even our 'dis'-beliefs, could
retain any value as revelations of the truth, for every
one of them without exception flows from the state of
their possessor's body at the time.

"It is needless to say that medical materialism
draws in point of fact no such sweeping skeptical
conclusion. It is sure, just as every simple man is sure,
that some states of mind are inwardly superior to
others, and reveal to us more truth, and in this it
simply makes use of an ordinary spiritual judgment. It
has no physiological theory of the production of these
its favorite states, by which it may accredit them; and

its attempt to discredit the states which it dislikes, by vaguely associating them with nerves and liver, and connecting them with names connoting bodily affliction, is altogether illogical and inconsistent."

This is an answer—perhaps *the* answer—to a question that has been plaguing me for the last 5 years: Is my brain churning out delusions beyond the norm or is my "crazy" life really happening?

It's happening. Thanks, Dr. James. Fantastic. Now how did I arrive there? Let us now dissect this.

I had a normal dream that involved some "alien abduction" related material. This may be a coincidence or it may be that whoever this mystery woman is either attached herself to the dream or produced it in me so that I'd draw the connection. Probably the latter. Probably there are implications about how these beings we call alien create circumstances that feel to us like missing time. But for the sake of this book, let's say that the woman interrupted my dream to speak a deeper truth using archaic English.

I woke up realizing this was not part of the dream. Her voice itself did not wake me up; it was the fact that what she was telling me made perfect sense whether awake or asleep. I don't know why but somehow this fact woke me up and I knew I had to jot down the utterance before I forgot it. I think I did lose part of that first line. However, it doesn't matter whether she said *thither* or *hither and thither.* What matters is that she did not use *there* or *here and there.* Had she said *there* instead of *thither*, it would not have made perfect sense to me, I would not have woken up and jotted it down, and I would not have searched it on the web.

The way my cynical brain works I would have heard "I understand there and in that understanding...." and thought it was nonsense. But saying *thither* is so odd that I had to look at it a different way. I looked at it as the *concept* of there or the *concept* of here and there.

The prose is about surviving death (physically or egoically, it matters not) as an independent entity by understanding deeply the illusion of space-time.

Why didn't she just say what she meant in the first place? Well the last time she tried that—during the I Am awakening—I ignored her because it sounded like idealistic blather. Furthermore, I wouldn't have looked it up online and found the answer to that material question of whether or not this is all a product of my brain.

I don't think it's too much of a stretch to say that my cynicism is one example of many and that the answers to all complex questions, from pollution to aliens to God, are one answer: It ain't really complicated. We complicate things because doing so means we can put off the solutions for another generation thereby continuing to live in hoggish comfort.

Take pollution for example. It's a no-brainer that the industrial world is destroying life on earth. I don't need a dream vision to tell me that. I don't need a female entity invading my headspace to lecture me on this, or in the event that I am conjuring the voice... well... I don't need to do that either. I'm aware of what's going on in the world politically and environmentally so unless this voice has a solid answer to pollution, shut up.

However, the solid answer truly is, "Stop polluting before it's too late." I can scoff at the simplicity of it all I want but there is no other magical solution. This is not complex. A guy like me brushes it off because it's so naïve, but that makes me a total dope because this is the answer.

See how uncomplicated it is? Cleaner energy is out there. Viable alternatives to paper exist. Solar power exists. Corporate and personal greed are the biggest roadblock to our survival. Our survival hangs in the balance because the answer to pollution, if not *stop polluting,* is *die.*

Do we get that? Pretty straightforward, right?

And that's true whether aliens are speaking to me, Mother Nature, or a splintered piece of my own persona. The messenger is not important even if the message sounds quaint. Thus far, here is what I've gleaned:

Our decimation of the ecosystem for creature comforts is almost beyond repair. We need to stop right now or we will die. There are other sentient beings in the universe who would help us but we deny their existence preferring confinement and suicide. The alternative, the only alternative, is to understand the illusion of separation and the truth of oneness.

Understanding of this type is not the same as understanding quadratic equations or the alphabet or how an automobile works. This understanding unlocks the body, freeing it of the ego's grip, thereby allowing real energy, real directive, real enlightenment to steer the human vessel. Only if we give over to that transcendental state will we survive death. Only if we become that will we stop blocking out other planets. Only if we become that will we join the universe of other like-spirited people who have chosen life over death.

To remain as we are is death. To say it's human nature is to lie before dying. We are not living out human nature because the ego state through which we define ourselves is unnatural. The ego is a tool of the Highest not the Highest itself.

How do I know this?—Because I've always wanted to remember.

Why am I remembering this now?—Our decimation of the ecosystem for creature comforts is almost beyond repair. We need to stop right now or we will die.

Evil aliens are not doing this to us. Evil politicians are not doing this to us. The devil isn't making us do it. This one's on us. All of us. If we remain ego-dominant creatures we will never correct our misdeeds no matter how altruistic the intention of our replacement systems.

Will we take that secret to our early graves?

***

The ethereal woman's comical, poetic, mystical, downright silly communication is not a product of my delusional brain. It is real and it is urgent. As of this writing, the lines are still open and so we must still have enough time to exact appropriate change or why would this woman bother? We now know what kind of change is needed and there is no future generation to whom we can hand the problem.

Let's do it now lest we die into the procrastinator's dream speciously called *hope*.

I Just Realized Something

As I reread *Hither, Thither, and Yawn* I realized something. Remember how I was all, "This book is an experiment the likes of which has never been done before, blah-blah...." Well, yes it has. I can't believe I didn't see it until just now but since just now is all we have that's the perfect time to notice. What do the following two messages have in common?

"Do we humans not understand that other planets cannot help us if we continue to block them out and kill ourselves?"

- And -

"I understand hither/thither and in that understanding shall neither be swept away nor carried on the seas of time."

Give up?

Both are in the first person. When I repeat them I am forced to repeat them as if I said them. When you read them you are forced to read them as if you wrote them. This was confusing to me after the I Am experience and led me to wonder if the woman who said it was Lisette Larkins. I wondered if the aliens were us in disguise and, as always, wondered what was the point of our interaction.

Unbeknownst to me, I would end up writing a book—this book—that employed the same instruction: To read it in the first person, to internalize it in such a way that it bypasses self and fosters enlightenment in the brain.

And here all this time I thought I was the genius doing the experiment. Once again, the joke is on me. Once again, we're all in this together.

Once, always, and ever again, together we are this.

I Be Trippin'

We have one more thing to discuss before I outstay my welcome. Although I'd always prided myself on never doing an illegal drug, in summer 2009 I broke my pride to partake in an informal hallucinogen experiment.

I co-host, with Jeff Ritzmann, an internet radio show called, *Paratopia*. Jeff and I are both "alien abductees." Notice how I tend to put that in quotes when referring to my own experience? It's because the term doesn't do the experience justice. I know that's the term popularized in the media but it really has no meaning.

Many abductees prefer the term "experiencer." Personally, I don't care so long as the point that comes across is this: we don't know what alien abduction is. In other words, Jeff and I, amongst others, are not at all certain what abductions are, but much of the phenomena described happen to us. Little doctors from another planet? Space brothers?

No.

Not that you'd know it from the media portrayal, but the evidence does not suggest this. These stories were pieced together from a larger data pool based on researchers' prejudices, their wrongful use of hypnosis for memory retrieval, and on what they thought the media would find acceptable. We can wrap our minds around alien doctors. Little people just like humans but more technologically advanced makes sense. *Star Trek* makes sense. Unfortunately, it doesn't make sense of what's happening to Jeff and me, so we decided to test the alleged correlations found in drug culture.

***

Leading up to our hallucinogen experiment Jeff and I read the research of Dr. Rick Strassman, Terrence McKenna, Dr. Dennis McKenna, Graham Hancock, and others.

The lab work of Dr. Strassman alongside the personal experiences of the other three researchers gives anecdotal evidence that alien abduction experiences can be produced by 1.) ingesting psychedelic substances, and 2.) triggering DMT overproduction in the pineal gland (not coincidentally identified as the *third eye* in various spiritual traditions).[7] Their research also suggests that hallucinations are not merely misfiring neurons in the brain producing delusions. Therefore, the term "hallucination" is as limiting as the term "alien abduction."

What DMT truly does, these researchers agree, is give one access to other freestanding realities the way television gives one access to different channels. All well and good except for one tiny detail: None of their work included abductees. How could they equate what was happening to subjects tripping on DMT with what happens to abductees when we weren't represented in the experiments?

Jeff and I decided to take matters into our own hands for the radio show and do some psilocybin mushrooms. Jeff, like me, lived a drug-free life up to that point. This would be a shock to both our systems.

Viva la science!

***

The majority of my trip, while interesting, isn't worth relating here—although I shall put you out of your misery and tell you that while we found parallels between the DMT-induced state of mind and what we call the *high strangeness* feeling associated with "alien abductions," they were not the same thing. One could argue that there are also equal parallels to the state of mind you're in right now and alien abductions or the DMT trip. Parallels to all states of mind abound because they are interrelated.

---

[7] DMT stands for Dimethyltryptamine. It is the hallucinogenic chemical compound found in numerous plants as well as the human body.

Oh, also—Hey, kids! Don't do drugs. Is it too late for that disclaimer? I've heard horror stories. Mindset and setting are everything. Common wisdom holds that you never trip alone and preferably do it with someone sober and experienced in hallucinogens to watch over you. You might trap yourself in a nightmare if you're not careful. So be careful. And... don't do them.

Disclaimer over.

I did far more 'shrooms than Jeff and triggered the kundalini energy upon ingesting them. The energy guided me through a long ordeal involving images, virtual realities, and a host of amazing things irrelevant to this book. However, there is one relevant facet of the journey for which this is prelude: At one point I entered Krishna consciousness. That is to say, in one instance my consciousness merged with that of the archetypal blue boy Hindus refer to Krishna. His is a ticklish universe of lively fractals, symbols, mandalas, and ecstasy that consume and become you.

Here's what's important to note: had I not first gone through the I Am experience I most certainly would have thought this was it. I would have thought this merging with Krishna consciousness was the great awakening. Visually, of course, it wasn't the same experience by any stretch, but there was also a nuance that you don't understand if you have nothing to compare with it. That subtlety is this: The ecstasy you feel in Krishna consciousness is like being tickled with a feather, as opposed to the I Am experience, which is like understanding all levels of a fantastic joke. In both cases you're laughing but one is harsh and gets annoying after a while. The other is deeply satisfying.

The bliss of Krishna consciousness happens *to* you. The bliss of I Am *is* you. This deity delights in your delight and will do anything to draw you into him. While that may be attractive to some, I found Krishna an irritating deception. Dare I say it smacked of spiritual gluttony?

In fact, the cumulative total of my trip angered me. I expected something deeper than anything I'd ever experienced, and while interesting, it certainly was not that.

That, I had already experienced.

That, I had already become.

And that is what I let go to share this with you because it's not about me waking up to the stage beyond stages. It's about all of us doing so, for all truly is one.

One wakes up or all are lost. Enlightenment is not more or less complicated than that.

IN CONCLUSION
Putting It All Together. Totally.

If we cobble the pieces together, what does the next phase of human look like? Imagine, if you will, a timeless nonlocal intelligence that contains an organic aspect through which it experiences the local and time. This being flows within and without the body through an ethereal gill in the lower spine. Using the pineal gland as a third eye, she tunes into other realities be they in this universe or another dimension. Such a person uses the brain like a map, finds a location she wants to visit, and goes there. Perhaps she is physically anchored to one location at a time but astrally she can instantaneously move anywhere she perceives. Such is the speed of relationship and the power of nonlocal perception.

One wonders what she looks like to inhabitants of the other realms she visits. A ghost? An alien? A ball of light? A dream?

Does she retain an image of her form or is she invisible? Is it her choice? Can she have any influence on the beings she observes? Does that depend on how awake they are?

These are the new questions we will be born into and there are others. Others like, what happens to social structures in our world when we become this revised definition of human? What do we do for work? I have two insights that might help with these. The first is something I'd come to long before this energy flowered in me. Our job would be to seek out other species with the same enlightenment potential and steer them in indirect ways. Ultimately, they have to make the leap themselves, as did we, but we must help open them to it. Must. It's another choiceless choice, for it is an extension of the "one waking oneself up" principle.

The second insight is that we will not need food to sustain ourselves once we are God-alive and so that's a huge nail in the coffin of economy. I got a taste of this while meditating one fine morning years ago. I felt satiated all day long. I didn't eat or drink or feel the urge. It was as if this kundalini energy were converting to nutrient energy. I don't think it was *as if* that, I think it *was* that.

There is scientific evidence to back this up. BBCNews.com reports that India's Sterling Hospital put an astonishing claim of then-seventy-year-old Indian hermit Prahlad Jani to the test.[8] His claim? That he has neither eaten nor drunk anything in the past twenty years. "I feel no need for food and water," he said.

The hospital monitored Jani for ten days straight under constant video surveillance. His one-room living quarters for that time had a sealed off toilet and he agreed not to bathe. The only fluid to which he had access was a small amount of water to use as mouthwash. This was measured after each wash to make sure he spat it all out. In those ten days he neither ate nor drank nor passed human waste. Urine did form in his bladder but it was reabsorbed into his body.

Prahlad Jani wastes not and wants not. Other than that he is said to function mentally and physically like any other normal healthy person.

As a delicious side note, he claims that he can live this way because a goddess blessed him when he was eight. He wears a tiki mark on his forehead common among married Hindu women and his followers call him *mataji*, which means *goddess*.

***

---

[8] Khanna, Rajeev, BBC News, November 25, 2003, *Fasting Fakir Flummoxes Physicians*. Retrieved from: http://news.bbc.co.uk/2/hi/south_asia/3236118.stm

It's hard to imagine a world of us local folks living nonlocal lives. We'd believe it if it were an alien society but not human. Aliens we could suspend our disbelief for, but us? Really, us?

Why not us? How we got to be the way we are now is fantastical any way you slice it. Believe in a far-fetched creation myth? Believe everything just is? Believe in Darwinian evolution? Whatever you believe and whatever the case is are going to be equally jaw dropping, it's just that one is going to be correct.

Currently we are a species with a divided mind. The basic division is conscious/unconscious. Each division has several subdivisions with their own subdivisions. What happens when we mend that one initial division from which all others flow? What happens to cultures and societies when they become flavors of choice not compulsion?

Picture a group of undivided individuals immediately seeing the fallacy of maintaining cultures and societies. In so seeing they shed their national identities leaving the individual and the global. In this moment even the global identity drops and the individuality of the organism—the personality—becomes like a note in a harmony.

With all divisions revealed as the unnecessary illusions they are, humanity joins a broader ecosystem full of beings they'd blocked out as part of the package deal when they blocked Truth.

Joining that broader reality might not be all wine and roses. There are other potential problems I can think of when we do become our total selves. For instance, we don't know what will happen to the symbiotic archetypes in our co-created mind spaces. Will they evaporate like disengaged holograms? Will they take on independent lives of their own as formless awarenesses? Will they incarnate? Will their universes squeeze out of the human mind's birth canal into existence for all sentient beings with interdimensional luxury yachts to visit? Will I apologize to the New Age movement after rereading this paragraph?

What if we've co-created nightmare worlds with nightmare creatures? Are we responsible for the havoc they wreak?

If we were to merge conscious and unconscious would it be anything less than fantastic? What does one become when one is internally undivided and locality is a choice? Certainly we don't roll on as a war-faring species. We don't wonder when our next meal will come or what's on TV or which god is real. Can you imagine yourself so satisfied with merely being that you never grow bored, never lose yourself to the hunt for bigger and better entertainment?

Well, no you can't. You can't imagine that because it is not you. This world literally and figuratively at our backs is not you. It has nothing to do with you. This is why you cannot have a motive in becoming complete. The motive is that you want this utopian vision for yourself. But you don't get to exist in it any more than the monkey gets to exist in you.

Hopefully less.

***

Whether the experimental aspect of this book worked on you or not, this is where we are going. This, if we make it. Transcendence vs. suicide: that is our first and final choice. All of the glorious progress we make to put it off is masturbation. It's funny because most of the popular self-help gurus out there tell you to get real with yourself but if you ever did you'd abandon yourself immediately.

Imagine doing that. Imagine eons of mistake corrected.

Imagine allowing God to come home.